Copyright © 2016 by Debra Joy

ISBN: 978-1519498809

All rights reserved. No part of this publication may be reproduced, distributed, or transmitted in any form or by any means, including photocopying, recording, or other electronic or mechanical methods, without the prior written permission of the author, except in the case of brief quotations embodied in critical reviews and certain other noncommercial uses permitted by copyright law. For permission requests, write to the author, Debra Joy

debra@debrajoy.me

Design: Steve Demelo

Photos for Ground and Touch: Cheryl Himmelstein

Other Photos: iStock

Chlorine free ink.
Printed on acid-free FSC certified paper.

For Nancy

Contents

Introduction

What if you could be free of anxiety, feel peaceful and secure no matter what?

What if you had deep joy inside you whether life was going your way or not?

How would it be to experience unbounded love for all beings?

And what if it could be simple?

Would that be a life you'd want to live?

For the past decade I've been helping people create and live lives they truly love.

I would like to do the same for you.

I've always had a burning desire to help people. When I discover something great I love to share it; whether it's a recipe, a skilled teacher, a secret hike, or a new way of doing things that makes life better.

In the winter of 2001, I discovered something more valuable than anything I'd ever shared before. What I discovered was my true nature.

Unexpectedly all my thoughts and beliefs, personal story, physical self and identity dropped away. What remained was a vast peace, a quiet joy. It was like being in outer space, except that I was the space, as well as the universe within it. It was a state of oneness. And it was pure love.

I recognized that state of being as who I really am. I'd always considered myself to be my mind and body, experiences and stories. But I discovered I was so much more. Behind my hopes and fears, ideas, identity, and conditioning, there was eternal, cosmic energy. Wanting nothing. Empty, yet full of everything. It was pure awareness. Pure potential. This was my true self, free of the self I'd always thought myself to be.

As soon as I realized this state of awareness, I knew it had always been there. I had just been so caught up in my thoughts and feelings that I'd missed this state of being that was more profound and vast than anything I'd been striving for.

That discovery changed everything for me. I didn't stay in that state of awareness forever. But I learned that I could return to it at any time, using my body as a direct path back.

By accessing my true self through my body, even for just moments at a time, I've tapped into wisdom beyond my intellect, a kind of cellular knowing that has guided me through a rich and beautiful life. When I access that state I'm no longer lost in who I think I am. In that state there's no thinking at all.

It's freed me from worries and fears, even in times of crisis. It's calmed my nervous system and made me peaceful, even when things aren't going "right". It's enabled me to feel and express more love and joy.

Clients come to me for different reasons.

They want to expand their business, find true love or create balance in their busy lives. They want to get their art out in the world, increase their revenue, or ease anxiety and enjoy life more. They want to love and be loved.

Though I often help clients achieve their goals by providing expertise from my past experience, I mostly teach them to access their own inner wisdom and come to know their true selves through body-based practices.

When they access their own internal guide, they drop the ideas of what they should do and who they should be. They can master their lives, living successfully in society, without being a slave to it.

They become truly powerful.

That's why I want to share these practices with you.

To create this book I chose from the dozens of practices I've created or shared with clients for their different situations. So I want to share the most profound and simple steps that have consistently great results.

These steps create a solid foundation for accessing the peace and joy of your true nature through the pleasures of your body. They won't require you to set aside time from your daily life.

They can be easily incorporated into your every day activities, no matter who you are, or what you do. They aren't more things to do, but rather new ways to be with what you're already doing. These new ways can transform your life.

These practices have helped busy corporate executives, seasoned spiritual advisors, open-hearted yoga teachers, and busy single parents with no time to spare. They've worked for non-profit leaders, successful actors, and wealthy investors. I'm confident they'll work for you too.

There's nothing more powerful than your true self.

It's your essence; the beautiful cosmic core of you that gets expressed through your ever-changing body and evolving personality.

It's the pure love energy beneath your goals, ambitions, and cultural conditioning. It's unwavering peace and unreasonable joy, that's deep inside you, no matter what.

You may be thinking, "I don't feel peaceful, joyful, and loving all the time."

Me neither. I don't know anyone who does. But your true nature is like the calm eye in the center of a hurricane. I want to teach you how to reach that calm inside you more often and experience for yourself the pleasure and power it holds.

Life is full of change. It can be chaotic and scary at times.

Your moods, your relationships, your finances, even your body and mind, are constantly transforming. Life is always in flux.

Everything around you and within you can change, but your true nature stays constant, infinite, boundless, and timeless.

When you discover a state of loving awareness underneath all your thoughts, emotions, and physical sensations, you experience peace and joy, in happy times and sad, in chaos and calm. And that is powerful.

When you don't know your own true power you'll seek it outside yourself.

You'll try to get security from things like your job, looks, relationships, reputation, or finances. But bodies age, relationships change, and finances are rarely as secure as they seem.

When you rely on things that change to make you feel solid and secure, you can feel powerful when things are going your way, and powerless when they fall apart.

Your true nature is the only power that lasts. You experience it through presence.

There is so much talk now about being present, but what does it mean, and why should you care?

Your true nature is always and only experienced in the present. For your true state of being it is always now.

When you access it, you step off the roller coaster of feeling dominant and powerless.

You become truly powerful in a way that empowers others.

When you experience and share the power of your true nature, your impact becomes more profound than you can imagine while your life becomes easier and more pleasurable.

A simple way to become present is through pleasure.

We're all pleasure seekers. Yes, even you.

I'm not saying you're a hedonist. You're probably hard working, and do lots for others. Whether it's conscious or unconscious, you do those things because doing them makes you feel better than not doing them.

You may even do difficult, uncomfortable things ... for pleasure.

You go to the gym, stick to a diet, and work long hours, because it will either make you feel better while you're doing it, shortly after, or when you achieve the things you want in the long term; whether it's a paycheck, enlightenment, or a better body.

If you're a parent, you make a lot of sacrifices, but feeling good is still at the core of your actions.

You may wake many times in the middle of the night, not because you don't need the sleep, but because you love your children. It may seem selfless, but there's pleasure in it. Getting up to feed and care for your child feels better than letting him cry.

Even in your fatigue, you're comforted by the weight of your infant in your arms. You feel the warmth of his body against your chest. As you soothe him, your own body relaxes. Your breathing becomes deeper as you feel that little body expand and contract. Even though you're exhausted, the edges of your lips curl and your eyes crinkle as you listen to the content sounds of him sleeping once again.

Pleasure is an inside job.

While pleasure can be sought in many ways, it can only be

experienced inside you. The round rich taste of ice cream, the high soft whistle of birds singing, the rhythmic movements of your body walking, can only be sensed from within.

Pleasure needs awareness. You can eat without tasting. You can dance and have sex without feeling. Babies can laugh without you hearing, and the sun can set without you watching. There may be hundreds of potentially pleasurable moments in your day, but if you're not paying attention, you'll miss them.

When you miss the pleasure that's already in your life, you'll find yourself constantly seeking more. You'll be looking out to the world for satisfaction, where it can never be found.

These practices will create moment-to-moment awareness, and that can open the door for the vast, cosmic awareness of your true nature to reveal itself. Once you've glimpsed who you really are, it's easier to shed that mistaken identity you may be living in.

Pleasure is experienced in the present.

Pleasure generates feelings that can only be experienced when you're aware of your body in that moment. Even a pleasant memory becomes more than just a concept when you feel the sensations it creates.

1. To experience pleasure you must be present.

2. Through presence you can realize your true nature.

3. When you know you're true nature you are truly powerful.

That basically sums up this book.

You can take that and run with it. Do what you will. Or you can read more.

I'll happily guide you through some simple proven steps that can help you access your true nature, and know your own power.

You may feel that these practices are far too simple to make such a difference.

Many of my clients felt the same at first. This note I received sums up a common experience of resistance:

"Debra, I have to admit I'd been resisting the practices because they seem too simplistic to actually make a difference with the heavy stuff I'm dealing with. Thanks for continuing to push me. Now that I'm actually doing them, I'm amazed at how effective they are. Everything is changing, from my work to my sex life. And you're right. I'm feeling better in my body and making decisions is so much easier. Thank you."

It's totally okay if you feel resistance to the practices as well.

If you'll explore them and try them for yourself, you too may find that with just your awareness, your whole life can change.

The following chapters may help you achieve your goals, deepen your relationships, love yourself and experience more joy.

It is my deepest hope that they will also bring you back to your true nature and set you free.

How to use this book

Follow your own instincts. Honor the way you do things.

Read it from cover to cover. Each chapter builds on the one before it.

Open it up and begin wherever you like. The chapters are also designed to stand alone. They can be read in any order. Because of that you'll find a bit of repetition in some places, but it's all there to help you understand viscerally. You may be motivated to create your own practice. There's space for that at the end of each chapter as well.

I hope you'll experience this book, and not just read the words.

It will come alive for you when you incorporate anything that inspires you into your own life. You may read a chapter and that's enough to send you on your own path of discovery. Some of you may want more guidance.

At the end of each chapter I've included a few specific practices to support the theme.

These practices aren't meant to be prescriptive. They're here to help those of you who'd like some specific steps you can follow regularly to experience more pleasure and power in your life.

Personally, I struggle with generalities, theories and concepts. I learn kinesthetically. If I can't do something myself, which is always my preference, then I can learn through real examples and details. As many details as possible. Enough so I can feel it in my body.

Once I feel the subtleties of the details, then I can usually grasp the theory.

We all learn differently, and I've tried my best to honor what might be your learning style.

All of these chapters have come from experiments I've done on my own and with my clients. I've included real stories to help you.

It can be tricky to tell people's stories while protecting their privacy. So in every situation I've changed the name of the person. In many cases I changed their business to one that was similar in nature. Sometimes my clients are facing similar issues and whenever possible, I created composite characters, using the true details of each.

Even if you've never been a client of mine, you may recognize yourself in one of these stories and think I'm writing about you. That's because we tender-hearted humans are all dealing with the core issues of love and fear and the desire to discover who we really are.

BREATHE

"Your deepest presence is in every small contracting and expanding.""

– Rumi

You've been charging around accomplishing your *to do* list all day. Each step of the way your thoughts rushed ahead to what you needed to get done next. Finally you return home, drop your bags by the door, and sink into the couch. AAAAAAAAAH.

With the surrender of that sigh, your body lets go.

Tension escapes through your mouth as your shoulders slide down your back. Your chest relaxes, and your weight gives itself to the sofa. In the instant of that exhale you feel your breath move through your body, perhaps for the first time all day.

Feeling the pleasure of that sensation was enough to stop your thinking and become present for just a moment.

Becoming present is the easiest way to live a life you'll love.

When you're present, you merge with the sensuality of life. You'll taste the deliciousness of food, feel the tingling pulse of arousal in your body, and hear your own inner wisdom.

Through presence, you'll experience more space in your life. You'll feel more connected to yourself and others. It will enhance your relationships, and your sense of self.

You'll tap into your creativity, and have more focus. You'll have less fear and enjoy life more.

Through presence you can access your true nature. It will give you peace. The peace that's inside you always, is just waiting for you to notice it.

Meditation is a great way to become present. If the idea of sitting on a cushion to reach for nirvana, makes your skin crawl, or you just don't have time, don't worry. There are many ways.

It can be seductive to try to master complicated practices that make you feel like a spiritual superstar.

The mind loves challenging puzzles, and the ego loves a sense of achievement. We feel proud when we accomplish difficult tasks. Feeling accomplished in your spiritual pursuits can be a big fat trap that keeps you locked into a spiritual identity, full of rules, roles and goals. These ideas about who you should be might be the very barrier that keeps you from experiencing who you really are.

Breathing is the simplest and fastest way to become present.

Though your ego may resist it, the simplest approach to freedom is often the most effective.

Your body and mind aren't separate, but it can seem at times that they are. You can be so caught up in thoughts that you're only aware of the world in your mind. You "forget" about your body for a while.

Thoughts happen tens of thousands of times a day, bouncing between the future and the past. It's easy to become lost.

Since your body's always with you, you might as well use it as a portal back to now. The moment you become aware of your body breathing, as you feel the rise and fall of inhaling and exhaling, you become present.

You don't need to change your breathing to become present, just pay attention to what goes on inside you as you breathe.

Inhaling was the very first thing you did when you were born. Exhaling will be the last thing you do in your life. Your body knows exactly what to do, so you rarely give it any thought. But breathing without noticing is like having a magic potion in your pocket and forgetting to use it.

Peace is at the core of who you really are.

If you dove into the ocean you'd discover a whole other world you'd never know from the land; a world of colors, textures and shapes you've never seen before. You'd notice creatures moving exquisitely slow and others so quick you can barely track them. While storms and waves may rage at the surface, you'd experience the peace of being suspended in the calm of deep water.

Sitting on the beach where you're warm and dry may be comfortable, but you'll only know this other world by diving in.

That ocean is like your body, teeming with life and full of sensations. You'll feel waves moving through you, slow deep pulses, fluttering, throbbing, tingling and quivering, when you pay attention.

There's an orchestra of pleasure inside you, each movement playing its part. At the core you can sense a stillness that's the conductor of it all. It's that eternal peace from which all this movement flows. It's inside you all the time, like the eye of a hurricane, or the calm at the center of a cyclone. It's your true self.

Your core is peace, no matter what storms may be swirling around.

Noticing your breath is like sticking your toe in this ocean. Focusing on your breathing is a way to dive in deep.

With wars, poverty, and global destruction, kids to raise, and that deadline at work hanging over your head, it may seem impossible to be at peace. It might even feel selfish to try to feel peaceful when the world is full of strife. But you can only give what you have. So if you want to help bring peace to the planet, your neighborhood, or family, you have to find it in yourself first. Accessing your true nature, through your body, you'll realize your true power, which is unwavering peace and unreasonable joy regardless of circumstances.

When you let the power of this peace guide you, you'll empower others too.

Have you ever taken a walk in nature and felt more relaxed just being there? Nothing's changed in your life, but tension melts away for no apparent reason. You breathe deeper. You feel the simple pleasure of being where you are.

Maybe you don't get that feeling from walks in the woods, but you experience it when you pet your purring cat, watch your baby sleep, or sit beside a good friend who lets you be you.

What's happening is a transmission of energy. You're getting a "hit of peace." It infuses you and calms your nervous system.

Everything in the universe is energy, radiating its vibes out into the world. When you're around the peaceful trees and critters in nature, your pet, your sleeping baby, or calming friend, their cells communicate with yours and you become more peaceful too.

In that same way, you can bring more peace to the world simply by being at peace yourself.

If the stress of life is making you feel irritable, frightened, or tense, it's hard to imagine finding peace within, but like the calm below the stormy waves, it's in you all the time.

You don't have to try to become peaceful, you already are. You just have to allow it. The easiest way to do so is through your breath.

You've been brilliantly designed to handle stress.

Your autonomic nervous system is made up of the sympathetic system, which prepares you to act (fight or flight), and the parasympathetic system which calms you, (rest and digest). It controls your bodily functions such as breathing, heart rate, digestion, elimination, and sexual arousal.

If your life is threatened, if you're about to be hit by a car or chased by an assailant, your body responds by going through dramatic physiological changes instantly. Your breathing becomes rapid. Your heart beats faster. Stress hormones flood your body, making you incredibly strong and fast. Your body uses these hormones to fight or flee, and you return to normal once you're safe again. Actually, these short bursts of intense stress make you better than normal, boosting your immune system and building your muscles.

The problem is that your nervous system doesn't know the difference between real and imagined danger.

When you fear you can't pay your bills, worry you'll be late when you're stuck in traffic, or relive negative experiences from the past, your nervous system is activated in the same way.

When your sympathetic nervous system is activated in response to stress, your body prepares to act. You breathe faster. Your heart pumps blood away from your digestive and reproductive organs and into your arms and legs where you'll need it more. When you have chronic stress with no real danger to fight or run from, the discharge of this arousal may not complete properly. Your parasympathetic system, which releases tension and increases relaxation, won't be able to do its job and so you linger in a stew of stress chemicals.[1]

When you're trapped in chronic stress without release, your mind can become hyper-vigilant. You find yourself focusing on potential threats in your environment. You can even read your internal physical changes as signs of danger, and that keeps you hooked on the stress loop.

While the fast pace of urban living, toxic air, water and food, all contribute to your stress, the greatest cause is actually your thoughts. Your reactions to what's happening, or might happen, or didn't happen, or should have happened, are stressing you out the most.

Since thinking causes most of your stress, it may seem logical to just change your thoughts. But if you've ever tried to control obsessive thinking, you know how challenging it can be to diligently monitor your thoughts and replace them with better ones. It can create more stress.

That's not the only problem. You're not even aware of the tens of thousands of the thoughts your mind is thinking all day. They become like painted walls of your home surrounding you. Occasionally they catch your attention, but most of the time they melt into the background.

Rather than fight a battle in your brain by trying to replace "bad" thoughts with "better" ones, just bring your attention down. Simply by focusing on your breath you'll let go of thoughts.

When you jump off the carousel of repetitive thinking, you land in the exquisite freshness of the present moment.

You might lose track of your breathing and find yourself back up in your thoughts pretty quickly. That's perfectly normal. The moment you realize you're thinking, let it signal you to notice your breathing again. As you focus back on your breath, thoughts dissolve once more. Not forever. They'll return. But focusing on your breath can sweep them away each time. With regular practice you'll experience lasting benefits and more peace of mind.

You can try it now.

Pay attention to your breath moving in and out of your body.

Feel how your body expands and contracts with each breath. If it feels comfortable, close your eyes and focus your attention on the sensations for just a few breaths. I'll wait right here.

As you paid attention to your body just now, you became present to what was happening.

You may have jumped back into thinking quickly, but whenever you focused on your body you were right here in the now. Your breath may even have slowed down and deepened with your attention.

Your breathing can change your state of mind.

When you're relaxed your breath slows down naturally. This reinforces a state of calm in your nervous system. It all happens unconsciously, but you can bring about this same state of calm any time you choose.

In my early thirties I began meditating daily. It was a simple practice of focusing on my breath for 30 minutes each morning. This was a stressful time in my life, and meditating offered a few moments in which I felt at peace.

The lure of that peace was so profound that I began taking a few slow breaths regularly throughout the day, just to remember how good I could feel. That practice was pivotal when a few years later I became very ill.

I was bed-ridden for a while with agonizing pain and debilitating fatigue. This was just after the dot com market crash of 2000. When my doctor told me that I might never work again, I had to face the prospect of supporting myself from my dwindling investments.

There were moments when I would be swept away by a tsumani of worry. "Will this pain ever end?" and "What will I do when the money runs out?"

When I'd feel myself being pulled by the rip tide of dark thoughts into a sea of despair, I'd feel my feet on firm ground, my body expanding to take in air, and contracting to let it out. The sensations of my body breathing brought me back into the present moment, where I was safe.

Because I'd had years of practice to form this breathing habit, it became automatic, like riding a bike. Slow breathing and peace became my response to stress and illness.

I still had extreme pain. I was more tired than I'd ever been. My finances were disappearing fast. But I couldn't focus on my breathing and be overwhelmed with thoughts at the same time.

My suffering from worry ended every time my thinking stopped.

As I breathed myself into the present moment, I experienced the myriad of sensations in my body beyond the pain. I felt the expanse of space inside me, the throb of life, the tingling of fear and excitement. Even though illness left me with a smaller and slower life than I was used to, there was still much to enjoy.

I became more aware of the abundant life around me. I became more accepting of myself, others, and all of life. My relationships deepened. With this acceptance came more peace and more joy.

The peace within you is full of life.

If you want to live with passion and do what excites you, peace may seem like a hindrance. It's something you'll get to later, maybe when you're older, and have accomplished all you want to do first.

This kind of peace isn't a buzz kill, even if you're a thrill seeker.

We often confuse excitement with stress. We've become addicted to the rush of hormones fueled by stress and fear, even though this hinders our health, relationships and enjoyment of life.

Fritz Perls, Founder of Gestalt Therapy said, "Fear is just excitement without breath."[2]

While that statement may be a bit simplistic, fear and excitement share many physical sensations: tingling, jitters, contraction, buzzing, and a rapid heartbeat. It can be easy to confuse the two.

Once you decide those sensations mean fear, you can get caught in a downward spiral.

When your breathing is shallow it reinforces the stress response in your body, and that can add to your fear. When you focus on your breath and allow it to slow down naturally, you interrupt the chronic stress response and can experience more excitement and joy with less fear and stress.

Think of something you'd love to do, but you're scared. Maybe it's something you've never done before. The fear of it keeps you from trying.

Do you have a message or talent you'd love to share with the world? Do you crave the feedback of an audience responding to you, but dread getting up on stage? Do you want to ask that person on a date, but fear rejection?

Fear can keep you from stretching and growing. It can hold you back from giving of yourself and enjoying yourself fully. Breathing can help you feel the energy of excitement while calming your nervous system and curbing your fears.

Breathing makes everything better.

Obviously you're breathing or you would have passed out by now, but you might not be breathing as much as you think.

Are you reading this on a screen? If so, odds are pretty high that you've been holding your breath. In 2008, tech thought leader, Linda Stone reported that 80% of people working or playing in front of screens experienced temporary cessation of breathing, or shallow breathing. She called it screen apnea. The 20% who didn't experience screen apnea were people who'd been taught deep breathing exercises and used them regularly. That may be all the reason you need to try the practices below[3].

If you're thinking this doesn't apply to you, join the club, I didn't either until I paid attention. We're not aware of screen apnea when it's happening, but it stimulates our sympathetic nervous systems, putting us in a state of fight or flight.[3]

Have you ever noticed yourself getting anxious when you're texting or emailing?

You get irritated if a page takes too long to load, even though it's only a matter of seconds. You snap at someone who interrupts you when you're reading online. You type so quickly you're body is rigid with tension. Or you feel fatigue, as if the energy's being sucked out of you.

Breathing slowly while in front of a screen will calm your system, increase your focus, boost creativity, and energize your cells.

This can give you a great advantage in work and play. It can also bring more pleasure into each online interaction.

Breathing will make you stronger, more focused and energized.

Every part of your body is made up of cells. Each of these cells needs oxygen to create energy. No oxygen, no energy. It's as simple as that.

In martial arts I was taught to use a kiai with every strike. It's a shout that comes from exhaling forcefully. Your body automatically follows that strong exhale with an inhale. The kiai doesn't have to be loud, but it should be strong. It helps focus your energy and strength. Kiais ensure that you are breathing while you're fighting.

If you've ever learned how to shoot a gun you were probably taught how to breathe in a relaxed way to increase your accuracy.

Athletes, dancers, and singers are all taught how to breathe to make the best of their performance.

In all aspects of life, conscious breathing will up your game.

Breathing is sensuous.

If you pay attention you'll feel air softly caress the inside of your nostrils as you breathe. You'll notice the temperature change between inhale and exhale. You'll discover that no two breaths are exactly alike. You're not mechanical. Your body pulsates with life.

Breathing slowly and easily, you'll awaken to a world of sensations inside you.

You can feel your body become spacious with your inhale and relax with your exhale, in rhythm with the pulse of the universe, but in a way that's uniquely your own. Breathing into your pelvis brings your awareness to your sexual and creative center, throbbing with life.

Every breath is a chance to let go completely and receive deeply; a practice that may translate into other areas of your life as well. You'll experience more flavors of your food as you inhale the aromas. You'll linger in the lusciousness of arousal longer as you breathe while making love.

Breathing will transform your relationships.

In many conversations people think about what they're going to say while the other person is talking. When you do that you're not really paying attention to who you're with.

If instead, you feel the expansion and contraction of your breathing while you're listening, you'll be more present with others. You can't feel your breathing and be lost in your thoughts at the same time. By noticing your breathing, you'll become a deeper listener. People will feel heard. This is one of the greatest gifts you can give a person.

When it's time for you to speak, you'll be more relaxed. Because you're more present, your thoughts and words will bubble up from a fresher place, not stuck in the past or rushing ahead to the future.

I was helping a client prepare for a big conference where she hoped to make lots of contacts to grow her business. Even though she's an expert and well known in her field, she was nervous about attending this invitation only event. I did an experiment with her, using breathing as a way to calm her nerves and connect with people. I asked her to listen while I spoke about myself. When she just focused on listening to me she found herself up in her own thoughts the whole time.

Then I asked her to feel her feet on the ground and notice her breathing while I spoke. By doing that, she was less caught up in her thoughts and could hear me clearly. When I was done talking a fresh idea popped into her mind to support what I was saying.

By focusing on breathing (and grounding, which you'll experience in the next chapter), she was less self conscious and better able to connect with me, from an authentic and spontaneous place.

When you first start to feel your breathing it may be shallow and fast. Your body might feel tight and uncomfortable. Perhaps you'll even sense a buzzing or tingling sensation. That's because shallow, rapid breathing can create anxiety in your system. When you feel that stress, your impulse may be to distract yourself and ignore these sensations.

That's understandable, but retreating to your thoughts won't give you peace that lasts. It will just keep you in the grip of compulsive thinking and reinforce the neural pathways in your system that were created by stress.

Staying aware of your body's sensations when you feel this

uncomfortable is probably the last thing you'd want to do, but if you'll try these following gently steps you might be amazed at your body's ability to shift out of anxiety and back into peace.

It would seem like the obvious solution to shallow breathing is to take a deep breath, but I've noticed that when given that direction, some people suck in a r, puffing out their chest and shoulders, and then force air out through their mouth. Over breathing like that can ramp up your anxiety, rather than diffuse it.

A gentle way to ease yourself out of anxiety, is to slow your breathing down. The simplest way to slow it down is to breathe through your nose. That might be enough to calm you.

You can further slow your breathing by bringing your awareness down. Where attention goes, energy flows. The easiest way to bring your attention down can be to feel your feet touching the floor, or if you're sitting feel your bum touching the chair. Sense the chair, and the ground, supporting you. It's important to not just think about that connection but let yourself really feel where your body is connecting with what's beneath it. Just by feeling that support your body may relax. That simple shift in your awareness can be enough to coax your breathing down. Your diaphragm contracts down as you inhale, creating more space in your lungs. Your downward focus can help support this action, and at least stop you from interfering with it.

I met a young woman who was a chronic shallow breather. She'd been studying with a teacher to learn to breathe deeply, but no matter what she tried she couldn't break out of her habit. I asked her to stop thinking about her breathing for a minute. I knew she had a young child, so I asked if she could remember what it was like to feel the weight of him inside her when she was pregnant. She could. I invited her to remember that sensation as she was sitting in the chair right now. I asked her to feel the chair she was sitting on, and imagine the weight of her baby pushing her body into that chair. After she did that for a few moments, I asked her to notice her breathing again. She was shocked that just by focusing her attention down into her pelvis her breathing had deepened effortlessly.

Feel what's happening in your body, low down, and notice what your breathing does.

Inhaling increases your heart rate and exhaling decreases it. This is natural and necessary. In times of effort or danger your heart will beat faster. When you're safe and relaxed your breathing and heart rate will naturally slow down. This slower pace reinforces a state of calm in your nervous system. When you're stressed, you can help calm your system by noticing your exhale.

As you breathe through your nose, allow your exhale to go all the way to its natural completion without forcing it. You don't have to squeeze out every last drop of air. That can create anxiety. The key is to allow it. At the end of your exhale, you'll feel air come back into your lungs through your nose and down into your body.

After you've exhaled completely and noticed air flow back in, keep breathing through your nose with a gentle focus on the subtle sensations of your natural breathing. You may feel a pause at the end of your exhale and/or inhale. Just notice and allow it.

Imagine a baby or animal sleeping. That gentle transition from inhale to exhale that fills your body with air and releases it is what you'll feel inside.

If shallow, rapid breathing is fueling your anxious state, allowing your breath to slow down gently can be a simple path back to peace.

What you'll find as you focus on your breathing is that before you know it you're back up in your thoughts. In fact you may be completely lost in your thoughts, unaware that you're breathing at all. It happens to all of us. As soon as you notice that you're thinking, let that be a prompt to focus again on your breathing.

Congratulate yourself for noticing because the moment you notice that you're thinking, you're no longer lost in your thoughts. At first, you'll be aware of your thoughts. Over time you'll realize that you are the awareness that's noticing thoughts. That vast state of awareness is your true nature.

It can seem like the solution is to wait until you feel overwhelmed, stressed or afraid and then breathe slowly as soon as you notice it.

Breathing slowly will shift you out of those situations, but by the time you're overwhelmed, stressed or afraid the older unconscious, reptilian part of your brain is calling the shots. And remember its focus is survival. That's not a time to learn something new.

Waiting until you're stressed to start breathing is like jumping off a boat in the middle of the ocean to learn to swim.

You'd most likely panic and maybe even drown. It would be much better to learn to swim in a safe environment and practice until your muscles knew what to do without thinking. Then you could jump off a boat, go for a swim, and enjoy yourself. That's exactly what I recommend you do.

Notice your breathing regularly until it becomes a way of being. You can use the breathing exercises at the end of this chapter until they become a habit.

The practices are so simple that you may dismiss them (remember - your ego loves complexity.) But their simplicity is part of their power.

With regular practice of simple slow breathing you'll create profound and peaceful changes to your nervous system. Your automatic response to life will become more relaxed, pleasurable and joyful. You'll experience more of who you really are. Like the runner's high, it's hard to imagine until you've experienced it for yourself.

I've had a myriad of weird health experiences throughout my life. For a few years I had little brain blanks. I'm not sure what else to call them. I'd be on one of my long walks around Santa Monica and suddenly I would have no idea where I was. Nothing looked familiar. As soon as I went blank I'd feel my feet on the ground where I was standing and breathe slowly, before I had the chance to panic. I didn't know where I was, but by feeling my body I knew who I was. I was peaceful energy, aware of what was happening.

There was no conscious effort on my part to remain calm.

I'd look around with curiosity, as if seeing the trees and buildings for the first time. Eventually everything would come back to normal and I'd realize where I was. Sometimes I was on my own street.

These times could have been cause for alarm, since I was aware that my brain wasn't "working as it should". But by creating a habit of easy breathing over the years, it had become my automatic response to stress.

You can achieve success by doing less and noticing your breathing more.

My clients come to me because they want to change something in their lives and haven't been able to do it on their own. They want something different, something better.

As well as offering my expertise in different fields, I offer simple exercises that help them access their own wisdom and experience the peace of who they really are.

I'm like the Wizard of Oz—not the scary great and powerful Oz who sends you on harrowing tasks to prove your worth. I'm the little guy behind the curtain who shows you that you had what you were looking for inside you all along. At times we all need little wizards to help us find the path into ourselves.

Maureen ran a multi-faceted wellness business that was growing in different directions. Each aspect brought varying levels of satisfaction, income and stress. No single division of her business was generating enough revenue to be sustainable on its own, so she kept them all going, dividing her focus and feeling overwhelmed.

She wanted help determining where to put her energy for the best results.

Fortunately, Maureen was very connected to her body. I guided her through a process of using her breath to feel which aspects of her work were most nourishing to her and the business. By breathing regularly and giving her energy to those tasks, she was able to focus more effectively.

Whenever she felt overwhelmed, she would breathe, calm down and decide what to do. By her sixth session she was clear on which aspects of the business she would focus on, which she'd delegate, and which she'd drop. She was able to let go of a lot, and focus on what mattered most.

Maureen emailed me saying, "I had no idea I could achieve so much by doing less and breathing more."

She was able to access her own inner guidance through breathing. In her following six sessions it was easy to develop systems for her life and business that suited her natural rhythm and gave her more pleasure and more money. She decided each next step by breathing deeply first, and listening to her own internal guidance.

Operating from that nurtured, self-directed place, Maureen felt empowered and calm. As she focused her energy on her passions, bigger opportunities came her way, opportunities she might have missed if she'd been buried under a hundred urgent things to do, holding her breath, in a state of overwhelm.

Breathing can show you your truth - the $50,000 breathing exercise.

Jocelyn and I have a quick call every week to focus on her priorities. She has a successful consulting business doing great work in developing countries. She was about to ask a funder for $150,000 to fund the next stage of her work. She felt a little nervous, but she was prepared to do it.

Rather than talk about it, I guided her through a breathing process that took about three minutes. After that I asked her, "What's the right amount to ask for?" She responded with great clarity, "$200,000". She was certain. By taking three minutes to breathe, she'd found her truth.

She wasn't attached to receiving that much. She just knew for sure that it was the right amount to request. She could feel in her body the extra "breathing room" that $50,000 would give her organization. She no longer felt nervous, even though she was going to ask for more.

It was her job to ask for it. The decision about how much to give was someone else's job. That clarity, that sense of power and lack of attachment to the outcome, put her in a great state to ask for what she wanted.

The funder said yes to $200,000 later that day. Those three minutes of breathing were worth $50,000.

The breathing techniques that follow are simple enough to practice every day no matter where you are, or what you're doing. They're powerful enough to guide you to the peace and joy that are at the core of who you really are.

BREATHING

Practices

– Notice your breath –

By just noticing your breathing you'll become present. You may start to notice more sensations in your body beyond expansion and contraction. Stay curious.

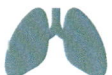 Feel your body expand in different directions with each inhale. Feel the contraction of each exhale.

 Just pay attention without trying to change anything.

 Do this for five breaths. If you lose count start at one again.

 Let your eyes look around once you're done.

Do this as often as you can throughout the day.

If noticing sensations in your body becomes overwhelming, go to www.debrajoy.me/resources for the Resource Guide. You can find professional help there.

- BREATHE ON CUE -

 Set the alarm on your phone or watch to ring three times today (more if you like).

 As soon as you hear the alarm ring, feel your feet touching the ground and take five easy breaths through your nose.

 Let your eyes look around when you're done.

 Notice how you feel.

The ringing of your phone may irritate you at first. That's not a bad thing. You'll be teaching yourself to respond to irritation with a calming breath. If you can't breathe for five breaths when your phone rings then just do as many as you can. Even one breath will make a difference.

If you miss the alarm just breathe as soon as you notice that it rang.

Allow your exhale to complete without forcing it. If you push the exhale too much you'll put your body in survival mode and gasp your inhale. You want a gentle transition from exhaling to inhaling through your nose without trying. If you notice a pause after your inhale or exhale, just allow that to happen.

If you keep your attention low in your body you can encourage your breath to slow naturally.

– TRIGGER YOURSELF TO BREATHE –

Choose one thing that you do many times a day:

- Stand up, send a text, pee, open an email, stop at a red light.

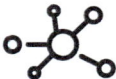
Choose just one.

Breathe every time you do that throughout the day.

- Keep your attention low in your body to encourage your inhale down.
- Breathe through your nose.
- Allow your exhale to be complete.
- Allow your inhale to gently follow.

Notice how you feel.

You'll be tempted to choose a few triggers because more is better, right? Not in this case. You'll develop a habit more easily if you focus on one simple thing, and repeat it over and over.

– USE STRESS TO FIND PEACE –

The moment you notice you're thinking a stressful thought - any thought that doesn't feel good - feel your feet touching the ground if you're standing or your bum touching a chair if you're sitting.

Focus on your breathing. Don't try to control or change your thinking.

Breathe through your nose. Let your exhale be complete. Feel your inhale gently follow your exhale.

Keep your focus in your body for several breaths. Notice how you feel.

This practice will be much easier once the earlier practices have become a habit for you.

Most of the time, when you're caught up in stressful thinking, you don't even recognize it. The moment you become aware of it you've separated yourself from it.

You may notice that as soon as your attention drifts away from your breathing the thinking is back. That's totally ok. You developed this conditioned thinking over decades. It will take time to develop a new habit.

Rather than resist it or be angered by being back in your thoughts so quickly, which only adds to your stress, see it as a cue to ground and breathe slowly again.

In this way, each stressful thought becomes a "coach" reminding you over and over again to get out of your head and into your body, where the present moment and true pleasure live. That's cause for a celebration. So the next time you realize you're thinking stressful thoughts, smile. And BREATHE.

– YOUR PRACTICE –

WHAT:

_____

Name this practice

WHY:

_____

_____

What do you expect to gain from this practice?
Knowing why you're doing it will help keep you motivated.

BREAK YOUR PRACTICE DOWN INTO VERY SIMPLE STEPS.

1. _____

_____

2. _____

_____

3. _____

_____

4. _____

_____

TRIGGER:

_____

When developing a new habit it's best to do it every day, at the same time if possible, and it's
important to have something that reminds you, or triggers you to do it.

What will trigger you to do this practice?

- NOTES -

GROUND

"SOMETIMES NEED ONLY TO STAND
WHEREVER , AM TO BE BLESSED."

– MARY OLIVER

When you live up in your head, life may be full of thoughts and ideas, which can be exciting or full of worries and fears, which creates anxiety. Living in your head keeps you bouncing between imagining the future and reliving the past.

When your attention drops down into your body you live in the present, where true peace resides. One way to do this is by grounding. You can ground wherever you are.

As you're reading these words, you can focus on them, judge them, or wonder what comes next. By doing this you keep your attention slightly outside of yourself.

Or you can bring your attention down.

If you're sitting while you're reading this, see if you can bring your attention to the feeling of your bum resting in the chair. Focus on that connection. What do you feel?

You may discover that you're not fully relaxing.

Maybe you're tensing your leg muscles unconsciously, to hold yourself up. I notice that often. Now that you're aware you can make an adjustment if you'd like. If you want to let go of tension, imagine your next inhale going into the tight muscles. On your next exhale allow them to let go. You don't have to force anything. Just allow the muscles to relax if they're able. You'll feel yourself let go into the support of the chair.

When you bring your attention down into the place where your body connects with the support below you, you're grounding.

When you ground in this way, you become present. When your focus drops down, your breath naturally deepens. It relaxes your nervous system, and gives you a break from the non-stop loop of thinking.

By grounding while you read, you'll experience these words in a different way. You'll feel the meaning in your body, as well as understand them with your mind.

Presence, experienced through your body, is where your true power lies.

I have a quick mind, and have lived most of my life up in my head. I've spoken quickly, grasped things quickly, and at times jumped to conclusions too quickly. I've been active most of my life, rushing through my days, my head stretched out in front of my body, trying to get there faster. Always pressing against time.

I was upbeat and excited, but underneath my happy personality I was unsure of myself. Easily influenced by other people's opinions, I wasted time wondering what they thought of me. I wasn't always aware of my own underlying uncertainties, but they directed a lot of my actions unconsciously. I never felt like I was enough.

All that changed when I moved to a little village in Mexico. I spent my days living at the pace of nature, and discovered my own true rhythm.

The town had no cars and was only accessible by boat. I'd walk to the store in a sarong, feeling the heat of the earth warm my soles. Though I was alone, the ever-present support of the earth's surface made me feel secure. Climbing the hill back to my house, my calves contracted as my feet pushed against the solid earth. Standing on the cool kitchen tiles on hot days, my soles relaxed into the soothing ceramic, refreshed by its touch.

Feeling the textures and temperatures through my feet filled me with some simple pleasures of being in a body full of sensations, even though I was dealing with chronic pain at the time. Focusing my attention down to the earth beneath my feet brought me into the present moment through my body. It freed me from the suffering of my fearful thoughts about the pain: "Is it going to get worse?" "How much longer will it last?" and "What's the cause of it?"

We often interchange the words pain and suffering. I'd like to make a distinction simply from my experience. My physical pain is an experience in the moment. Though chronic, it's not constant or static. It changes and ebbs and flows.

Though I prefer being pain free, pain isn't the cause of suffering for me. Suffering comes when I get lost in thoughts about the pain, worry about it, and wish it was different. The suffering comes from resisting what's actually happening, rather than experiencing it in the moment.

Worry stops when I bring my focus down. Grounding is a way to bring an end to suffering.

Grounding makes you strong.

In Mexico, my yoga practice grew more powerful from grounding. I drew strength and balance from the connection between my feet and the earth upon which I stood. I began each practice by feeling my connection to the ground, like a tree sending its roots down into the earth for nourishment. I would imagine the earth's energy moving up through my body, elongating my spine, and filling my muscles with its pulsing life force. This daily yoga practice strengthened me in a way I hadn't experienced back home.

As my connection with the earth grew, my breathing deepened.

No longer living up in my head, I embodied my belly and legs more. Feeling rooted in the natural world, life felt more abundant, varied, and sensuous.

By grounding, I found my natural pace. I moved slower and softer than I had in the city, as I felt the ground beneath my feet. I felt the textures of nature surround me like a soft blanket. They filled my senses with the sights of birds and flowers, the sounds of donkeys braying and children laughing, the smells of fresh tortillas in the morning, and ylang ylang flowers blooming at night.

I could feel myself in the midst of it all, and a part of it all. I was becoming a woman with hara.

Hara is a Japanese word for the space below your belly button. It means more than gut or belly. It's said that someone with Hara is grounded. She knows who she is and where she stands.

When the winds of tragedy struck me, as they did in that little town, I was able to bend without breaking, like a well-rooted tree. The shock of trauma made me want to collapse, but because I'd been practicing grounding for some time, I breathed deeply, felt my connection to the earth, and stayed standing.

Living in an open-air house, in a jungle surrounded by wildlife, helped me connect with nature. Walking through a village with no roads, cars, sidewalks or shoes, helped me ground. While it's easier to ground in more natural settings, I'm happy to report that I've imbued life in the city with the strength and sensuality of grounding.

You don't have to move to a remote village to become more grounded. At the end of this chapter I'll show you some simple steps to ground right where you are now.

Being grounded isn't something I would have craved before I experienced it for myself.

I thought people who were grounded were boring; slow to decide and even slower to act; gathering information, and analyzing the options. In my mind, grounded people were practical and dull. I was wrong.

When you're grounded you experience yourself in the present moment. While it begins with feeling your connection to the earth, it becomes much more than that. When you're truly grounded you feel comfortable in your skin. To be grounded is to be passionate, clear, and decisive. Grounding makes you stronger. You feel calmer and more empowered.

Think of a cougar on a tree limb, 15 feet above the ground. In that precarious position she's relaxed and at ease, sure of herself and where she is. She's grounded though she's not on the ground. She's completely present. When she sees her prey she pounces quickly and accurately. Her strong paws propelling her up to 50 miles per hour as she pushes off the ground.

When you're grounded it's easier to connect with the power of your own animal nature.

Grounding makes you supple.

You may think that being grounded will kill your spontaneity, or stop you from "going with the flow," but when you're grounded you'll move through the current of life with more grace and confidence.

If a boat is top heavy it can easily capsize.

It's the weight below the water that keeps ships upright when they're being pummeled by waves. You too can ride the waves of life, and weather the storms when you're grounded. But it's not just supportive in tough times.

You'll be able to handle more energy and excitement running through you.

When you plug electrical equipment into a wall, it's grounded through a metal bar that runs from the electrical outlet deep into the earth. If for any reason there is a surge of energy, the excess power is driven into the ground where it's dispersed. Without that grounding protection in place, a sudden bolt of power could fry your electronics from the inside, blowing out its circuits.

Think of your body like that equipment. When you're grounded your body can handle more energy. You'll experience a wider range of emotions, sensations, feelings, excitement and creativity moving through you ... without being overwhelmed.[4]

You'll become a conductor of greater power.

When you're not grounded, your body protects you from these overwhelming power surges by dampening down your felt sense of joy, ecstasy, and sexual excitement. These and other strong emotions, like anger and hurt, can stay stuck inside you, weighing you down.[4]

This all happens unconsciously.

You won't notice you're doing it, but you'll restrict your breathing, clench your muscles, or perhaps disconnect from your bodily sensations by living in your thoughts.

When you're grounded your body can handle more. You'll breathe deeper and your body will relax. You'll feel more expansive. Energy will run through you without getting stuck or blowing out your circuits.[4]

When you're grounded you're clear.

If we continue with the metaphor of electronics, grounding is vital for clarity. In recording studios, many types of equipment are used to create music. All of these pieces of gear must speak to each other. An electric guitar connects to an amp, which travels to the mixing board, and blends the guitar sound into the recording.

When a studio isn't properly grounded, the equipment doesn't send or receive sound clearly. Other "noise" gets picked up on the way.

The same is true for you. When you're grounded, your internal system of communication becomes more regulated. When you're grounded you're present. When you're present you know your own truth and can communicate it clearly.

When you aren't grounded, it's hard to hear your own wisdom.

You can get caught up in the ideas, dreams, memories, and critical thoughts buzzing through your mind. You get lost in the messages coming at you from outside. Your direction and communication can get muddled.

When you're clear the world responds to your clarity. You can be spontaneous, flexible, and strong, responding in the moment with what's true for you.

You become more confident and secure when you let the ground support you.

Often we don't even notice the things we do daily that cut us off from the earth.

We get mixed messages about how to be attractive to others. One prevalent message tells you to suck in your stomach and puff out your chest to look stronger and sexier, but holding your body this way can cut you off from the core of your sexual energy and primal nature.

Then there's fashion. In clothes that bind, pinch and restrict your movements, you'll numb out some of your feelings.

And who doesn't love a pair of sexy high heels? Wearing them can be fun. But they sever your connection to the earth, keeping you slightly off balance. Heels contort your spine. Your body wants to be properly aligned so your calves, hips, and back muscles tense in an attempt to you bring you back into your natural position. This stops you from fully relaxing into the support of the ground, and makes you more vulnerable.

When you feel cut off from the earth, you try to support yourself by tensing your body.

Without realizing it, you may hold yourself up by your shoulders. They're chronically creeping up towards your ears, rather than resting on your rib cage where they belong. You might clench your upper back, genitals, and rectum. You lock your knees and grip your thigh muscles. All of this happens unconsciously and creates chronic stress.

Your tight body acts as armor.

For a while that can make you feel safe. But that armor keeps you separate from nature, others, and even your own inner sensations. Without the connection that grounding provides, the world can be a scary, lonely place.

When you lose your connection to the earth and you're cut off from your primal nature, sexual energy, and natural rhythms, you'll override your intuition with rationalizing, worrying and second-guessing. You stop trusting your gut.

When you no longer trust your inner wisdom you'll look everywhere for things to make you feel safe and in control. Wearing the latest fashions, attending self-help workshops, and having a fat retirement fund might make you feel secure for a while, but they won't give you a peace that lasts.

When you allow yourself to be supported by the earth, you start allowing support in other areas of your life as well. As your body relaxes down, you can open more to what life is offering you. This enables more spontaneity.

The only true power comes from knowing who you really are. You can know yourself through your body. Grounding is a way to get you there.

Grounding brings peace.

A few years ago I worked with Carol, a woman in her mid 30s. She was healthy and beautiful with a handsome, successful husband, happy young son and a thriving business that she loved.

Through our work she began noticing the discomfort of anxiety that was always with her just under the surface—tightness in her chest and throat, rapid heartbeat, and worrisome thoughts looping through her mind.

The early stages of awareness can be very uncomfortable. Once she became conscious of this underlying anxiety she realized that it was the driving force behind her constant busyness and sense of overwhelm. Though she had what others would describe as an ideal life, she wasn't able to relax and fully enjoy it.

We first created a regular practice of grounding several times a day. It took a while for this to become natural for her. Once grounding became a habit, she learned to do it as soon she noticed any nervous energy in her body, and she'd immediately feel calmer.

Over time her anxious feelings dissipated. It's not that she was never nervous again, but it was no longer her chronic state. Without anxiety driving her thoughts and actions she stopped being hyper-vigilant, and started laughing more. She took some risks to pursue her dreams without questioning and second-guessing herself.

When anxiety returned, she knew how to bring herself back to the peaceful state of being present in her body.

Grounding creates connection

Janet had developed an enviable reputation as an expert in her field. It put her in demand as a public speaker. She loved the excitement of the crowd, the theatrics of presenting, and the money she made from big events. Nobody knew her material better, prepared as thoroughly, or had more passion for her subject.

There was only one problem. She would find herself on stage having raced through the material barely aware of what she'd said and done. She'd criticize herself harshly for days afterwards, replaying what she might have forgotten. Every time this happened it knocked her confidence down a notch.

Like many smart people, Janet lives a lot of her life in her thoughts. It took a while to convince her of the merits of grounding, but over time she became willing to try. She prepared and practiced her talks barefoot, bringing her attention down, feeling her connection to the earth.

She stopped wearing super high heels to presentations, and replaced them with shoes that let her feel stable. When she went on stage she'd take a moment in front of the crowd to feel her feet on the stage, let her body relax into the floor, and feel the support beneath her. Then she'd take two slow breaths.

She worried that grounding in front of the audience would be awkward and make her nervous, but it had the opposite effect. In the moment it took her to ground, she calmed herself and connected with her audience. Most importantly she connected with herself, where she was, and what she was there to do.

After her first attempt, she finished her talk more aware of what she had said. She knew she had really connected with her audience because more people came up and talked to her than ever before. They were interested in what she had said and wanted to know more. Over time grounding increased her enjoyment and eased her anxieties, which continued to improve her performance.

Grounding is sensuous.

Back when I was a personal trainer, Jean was a client of mine. She was a competitive dancer, moving up the ranks very quickly, but she couldn't break through to the highest level. By watching her dance I could see she was technically strong, but lacking sensuality.

She had studied ballet as a kid and done ballroom dancing in her 20s. These dances accentuate height, alignment, and posture, but they can lack the sensuality and rhythm of being connected down into the pelvis, legs, and the earth below.

Having never learned to relax down into her pelvis, legs and feet, Jean was tense with the effort of holding herself up by her shoulders. I could almost see the anxious energy around her head.

Alexander Lowen, the founder of Bioengertics says, "When we pull ourselves up and away from the lower half of the body, we lose much of our natural rhythmicity and grace."[5] While technically accurate, Jean's dance lacked feeling.

I recommended some breathing exercises to drop her awareness down into her pelvis. She started walking barefoot and squatting on the floor rather than sitting in a chair as much as possible, to feel her connection to the earth. I then sent her off to explore belly dancing and African dance to re-engage with the lower half of her body. It took time, but feeling the ground helped her access her sensuality. That helped her break through to new levels in her Latin dance competitions.

Whether you're dancing, walking, or sitting, grounding will connect you with the natural sensuality of your body.

Simply by feeling where you stand you can become present to who you are. You can incorporate the simple practices below into your daily life to experience more of the strength, grace, and expression of your true self.

GROUNDING

PRACTICES

– WAKE UP YOUR FEET –

You often don't notice your feet unless they hurt. This simple practice will bring awareness to your feet first thing in the morning. Starting your day with this practice will make it easier to ground throughout the day.

 As soon as you wake up, lie on your back in your bed.

 Let your feet hang just over the bottom of your bed.

 Spell the alphabet with your toes. Both feet at the same time.

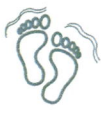 Notice the sensations in your feet as you move them.

This practice will also increase the range of motion in your ankles.

– GO BAREFOOT –

We spend so much time in shoes that we desensitize our feet, the very source of our grounding.[6]

Walk barefoot slowly enough to feel the textures and temperature of the floor beneath you.

Kick off your shoes under your desk and let your feet move.

Wiggle your toes, roll your foot around your ankle. Be expressive with your feet.

As often as possible, go outside to feel the moist grass, the hard sidewalk, or the gritty sand of the beach.

When your feet are lacking in life it's hard for your body to feel alive. Wake up your feet by feeling the ground beneath you.

– GROUND WHERE YOU STAND –

If you ground while you're standing, your body will naturally move towards alignment, improving your posture, energy, and mood.

 Bring your attention down into your soles and feel the texture of the ground beneath you.

 Inhale deeply, and on your exhale let your feet drop into the ground as if they'll leave a deep imprint of where you stand.

 Let the ground support you as you rise up and stand tall, keeping your connection through your feet.

 Standing with dignity, let your belly relax into your pelvis and your shoulder blades relax down your back. With each exhale let a part of your body relax down without slumping or slouching.

Do this any time you are standing - waiting for a bus, standing in a line, cooking dinner, watching your kids' soccer practice.

– FEEL F.A.B. –

You probably spend a great deal of time sitting. You might as well use that as an opportunity to ground and become present.

 Feel the texture of the ground beneath you through your feet.

 Notice all the places your body is touching the chair.

 Inhale deeply, and as you exhale drop down into the support, as if you'll leave a deep imprint of your body in the chair.

 Get comfortable and slowly scan your body from inside. If you notice any muscle that's gripping, trying to hold you up, inhale into that muscle and as you exhale from that place just invite it to let go.

Even though the chair or ground is perfectly capable of supporting you, you may be unconsciously "levitating above it" by gripping your muscles, rather than letting yourself relax into the support that's there for you. Don't try to force anything. Just invite your body to let go.

Your commute is a great opportunity to relax. It can help if you do this while driving or riding transit.

FAB can help you remember this.
F = Feet on the ground
A. = Ass in the chair
B = Breathe

– USE YOUR ROOTS –

This practice takes a little more focus, body awareness and time than the others. It's great to do when you need to feel strong, solid and energized.

 Begin by grounding through your feet, as you've done above, and breathe slowly and easily.

 Imagine the soles of your feet opening up and roots growing down from your feet into the earth. Send them deep and wide. Imagine the roots moving slowly, effortlessly through the ground beneath you.

 Receive energy from the earth up through your roots. Feel the energy moving up through the roots into your feet, filling your legs, pelvis and torso, energizing your core and arms, relaxing your shoulders, neck and head. Trust that the earth will send you exactly what you need from its limitless supply. Is the energy cool, moist, dark, bright, or warm? Pay attention as it moves through your body.

 Let this energy clear out channels as it moves through you. Let the energy push out any blocks you feel inside. Take your time.

Do it before a big presentation or event. If you're feeling sluggish or low try this before reaching for caffeine.

– LEARN FROM NATURE –

Nature is a very willing teacher. It will imbue you with a sense of being grounded, if you'll let it.

 Find something in nature that seems grounded to you. Even if you're in the heart of the city you can find a rock, a tree, or an animal.

 Let it teach you what it means to be grounded. Look at it. Touch it if you can. Sit beside it or on it. Lean against it.

 Close your eyes and imagine yourself as this being. How would it sit, stand, or move? How would it breathe? What would it think? What does it feel like to be this tree with roots going into the earth, or how does your body feel when it's as solid and still as a rock? What message might this being have for you?

 Any time you want to feel more grounded, embody that being again. Close your eyes to remember how it felt. Then let that energy direct your actions and your thoughts. Remember that energy when you feel anxious, confused, or overwhelmed.

We all imagined as kids, as a way of exploring different ways to be. Imagine yourself as this grounded being, embody it wholeheartedly, and you'll discover deeper, more grounded aspects of yourself.

– YOUR PRACTICE –

WHAT:

_____

Name this practice

WHY:

_____

_____

What do you expect to gain from this practice?
Knowing why you're doing it will help keep you motivated.

BREAK YOUR PRACTICE DOWN INTO VERY SIMPLE STEPS.

1. _____

_____

2. _____

_____

3. _____

_____

4. _____

_____

TRIGGER:

_____

When developing a new habit it's best to do it every day, at the same time if possible, and it's
important to have something that reminds you, or triggers you to do it.

What will trigger you to do this practice?

- NOTES -

44

TOUCH

"TOUCH ME. REMIND ME WHO I AM."

– STANLEY KUNIZ

What touches you has an affect on you that's more than just skin deep.

Hold a newborn's tiny feet in your hands...

...Walk on cool soft moss...

...Ease yourself into a hot bath...

...Scrape your knee on the pavement...

...Stand waist deep in a snow fed rushing river...

...Run your hands through an animal's soft fur coat.

Each of these moments will arouse a medley of sensations inside you.

Remember the last time you felt a warm embrace. Someone you trust put her arm around you when you were scared. Your lover ran his fingers across the back of your neck. Your friend hugged you and held on tight.

Your body softened. Your breathing slowed down and reached deeper inside you.

Touch has a way of calming you into yourself, while connecting you with another.

The stuff you experience as your body is packaged in a sensuous wrapping called skin. This pliable membrane is your body's largest organ that both separates you from the rest of the world, and gives you a delicious way to tangibly connect with it. It's sensitive and strong and wonderfully responsive.

Full of sensory receptors, this protective covering is your portal to textures, temperatures, and pleasures. It can also be the portal to your true self.

Skin is one of the ways that awareness (consciousness, God, Source, Shakti, Spirit) gets to connect with itself in its other forms. The hairs on your arm stand up as a cool breeze caresses you. The touch of someone makes your skin tingle. A warm blanket on your body relaxes your muscles.

These are all ways awareness embraces itself in its many forms. When you really pay attention to the sensations of touch it's hard to know where you end and the other begins. You can experience a sense of oneness through touch.

Touch is a basic human need.

It's the first sense you developed. Babies who aren't touched enough are more likely to die as infants. Others fail to thrive, never reaching their full height or weight.[7] You'll probably feel a visceral reaction if you imagine a delicate newborn not being touched.

When women have just given birth, the skin on their chest is a degree or two warmer than the rest of their body, creating a natural warming zone for the baby, what a snuggly miracle. The mother's body thermoregulates so that when the infant's body temperature drops, the mother's temperature rises and vice versa.

Babies who are held are calmer, sleep better and have superior brain development to those who aren't. Mothers who hold their babies experience reduced stress hormones and increased oxytocin, the bonding hormone.[8]

Children learn about their world through tactile exploration, discovering the temperature, texture, weight, fluidity and solidity of everything in their life through touch. Loving touch supports their growth, confidence, and willingness to explore.[9]

Those same benefits of touch apply to all of us, not just moms and babies. Nature has designed you for skin-to-skin contact.

Touch is a primary source of nourishment.

You already know the healing power of touch intuitively. When you hear your baby cry, your first instinct as a parent is to pick him up and hold him tight. You'll look for other ways to soothe him, but those ideas are secondary. It's your nature to touch for comfort first.

When you injure yourself you automatically touch the place you're hurt. You embrace people you love, and feel a deeper connection to them when you do.

Whether you're happiest at a raucous party with all your friends, or prefer quiet nights at home, you are a social animal. You're part of a species that interacts with one another to form a society.

All social animals need regular touch for optimal well-being.

Research shows that touching enhances the bond between people, leading to more open and honest relationships. A simple 20 second hug has the power to boost your oxytocin levels, reducing feelings of isolation and loneliness. It can relax your muscles, calm anxiety, and reduce your blood pressure.[10] And it's a lot more enjoyable than taking a pill.

We all feel alone and frightened at times. The warmth of someone's embrace can calm your fears and connect you not just to them, but also to the deeper part of yourself. It increases your serotonin levels, making you feel happier and boosting your self-esteem.

Sometimes when it's hard to find the right words to say, a touch can do so much.

There are times in life when you want to say the right thing but words don't come easily. You want someone to know you're there for them. When your words don't express enough, try touch.

We send and receive emotional signals through touch much more than we realize. We can detect distinct emotions like love, gratitude, sympathy, happiness, sadness, anger, and fear, solely through touch, with over 70% accuracy.[11] That's pretty accurate.

Because of this, touch increases your speed of communication. Laura Guerrero, co-author of Close Encounters: Communication in Relationships, says "If you're close enough to touch, it's often the easiest way to signal something."[12]

We were sitting in my friend's backyard, when her 10 year old son, Max, pushed his bike through the gate and went straight into the house. I've known Max most of his life, and it wasn't like him to shy away from a crowd.

When Adele and I got up to refill the iced tea and get desserts, Max was in the kitchen, with his head hanging down, avoiding eye contact. "What's up?" Adele asked casually, though I could tell she knew something was wrong. "Nothing" Max mumbled, staring at the ground, his body tense.

She put the plate of cookies on the table, leaned against the counter next to him, and casually slipped her arm over his shoulder. The tenderness in her touch seemed to open him up. He started shaking, and then crying. She quietly turned his body into hers and held him tight. In the safe embrace, his emotions freely flowed. His mom didn't tell him to stop crying. She just held him while he cried. It didn't last long.

Right after the emotions, the truth came out. A car had banged into Max while he'd been riding his bike. It had been moving slowly and he wasn't hurt, but it had shocked him.

The driver wanted to take him home, but Max didn't want to get into a stranger's car. He was afraid to tell his parents because he thought he'd get in trouble for riding on the road. He knew he was supposed to stay on the sidewalk.

Adele kept an arm resting on Max while he talked, and by the time the story was over he was able to look her in the eye.

Sometimes a touch can convey love and acceptance more than words. Adding touch to a conversation, even a difficult one, can help create and maintain a close connection.

Touch affects how you think and feel.

What you wear, sit on, walk on, lean against and hold in your hands can impact your thoughts and emotions without you even realizing it.

Research shows that the quality of objects you touch tilts your emotions and judgment towards those same qualities. Sitting in a hard chair can make you more rigid in negotiations, and touching a rough texture makes you more likely to judge harshly.[13]

The same part of the brain that registers physical temperature also registers interpersonal warmth. Holding something warm can make you feel warmer towards others; more trusting, and compassionate.[14]

Perhaps that's why some people don't want to talk until they've had their morning coffee. It's not just the caffeine that makes them more capable, but the warm mug in their hands makes them more compatible.

Next time you're getting dressed, consider how you want to feel, and wear clothes that touch you that way. Hold things that will help you feel warm, open, strong, or soft, depending on what you want.

If this is all getting a bit too touchy-feely for you, it's important to know that touch can be a secret weapon to your success.

Touch improves your mental and physical performance.

A touch can increase your speed and accuracy when solving problems. That's a good reason to get a big hug before you head to work or school. Maybe we should teach kids to shake hands, hug, or give each other a pat on the back before sitting down to write exams.

Psychologist Michael Kraus tracked physical contact between NBA players in the 2008 - 2009 regular season. He discovered that early season touch predicted greater performance for individuals and teams later in the season, even after accounting for player status, preseason expectations and early season performance.[15]

Touch enhances bonds, improves confidence, and increases cooperation between people. This can improve relationships and performance in families, at work, and on teams.

You'd probably benefit from getting a little more.

A litter of puppies scramble over each other, sleep in a pile, and play fight to develop their skills. If you have a dog, cat, or horse, you've probably experienced them unabashedly nudging you and pressing themselves against you for touch. They have no inhibitions about getting what they need.

When you pet them, groom them, and let them curl themselves around you, it's not just the animal that benefits. It has a settling, calming, and soothing effect on you. But sadly most teens and adults get less than half the touch they really need. This is partly because social inhibitions get in the way.

We've sexualized touch to the point where we're uncomfortable sharing a loving embrace, fearing its implications. While erotic skin on skin contact is a wonderful and natural part of life, we miss out on a whole world of sacred connections if we limit touch to romance and sex.

Living without touch can make you feel alone and unloved, like there's something wrong with you. This can lead to shame and isolation. This basic human need becomes a longing inside you that you keep bottled up.

It's painful for any of us to feel a need that goes unmet, like a deep hunger with no food in sight.

Even though all humans have needs, touch is one that can make you feel vulnerable. So rather than sense the longing for touch, you may shut yourself off from your own feelings. You can do it by taking shallow breaths, disconnecting from your body's sensations, and experiencing life primarily through your thoughts.

While it may seem as if this keeps you safe from the pain of your longing, it also cuts you off from your own humanity and the pleasures of your body. You can't block out "bad" feelings without suppressing "good" feelings too.

The answer lies not in denying your need for touch, but by embracing it.

It all starts with paying attention.

Rather than looking for new ways to touch and be touched, become aware of all the ways in which touch is already happening in your life. Awareness is the first step of transformation.

Take a moment to close your eyes and notice ways and places you are being touched right now. Feel the weight and texture of your clothes against your skin. Sense the temperature of the air touching your body. Feel the warmth of light on you. Notice the heaviness of this book or tablet in your hands.

When you're walking or standing, feel your feet touch the ground. If you're sitting in a chair or lying in bed, feel all the places it holds the weight of your body. Let your body drop into that support and feel yourself being held.

When you start feeling the touch that is already in your life, you'll welcome more touch in.

If you'll feel the many ways you're being touched each day, you'll awaken to the hundreds of sensuous pleasures you've been missing: water pounding against your body in the shower, silky lotion gliding over your skin, a cold wind blowing your hair, sunshine warming your face, delicious tastes stimulating your tongue, and air caressing the inside of your nostrils every time you breathe.

As you feel the ways you're being touched, your body eases, almost as if you're being hugged.

You'll discover that your breathing becomes deeper and your muscles relax. The chatter in your mind calms down. The feeling may only last as long as you're paying attention, but the more often you notice, the longer the benefits will last.

Your body is designed to feel. It takes a lot of unconscious energy to block out touch. When you let yourself feel all the ways you're being touched, you free up a lot of energy in your body and in your life.

What's touching you is always affecting you.

As you pay attention to things touching you, you'll notice that some things don't feel very good. You may suddenly realize your waistband is pinching your sides, or your feet hurt from the angle of your heels. You may be uncomfortable in all sorts of ways.

If you allow yourself to feel the discomfort, you can start making simple changes to feel better.

You may upgrade your office chair, start wearing breathable fabrics, drink your morning coffee from a hand-made mug, or swap your body lotion for something smoother.

Small changes can have a big impact on how your body feels, and how you feel about yourself. And that can change everything.

It can also change how you look. I once heard a doctor say the best thing a woman could do to avoid wrinkles was to wear comfortable shoes. Discomfort will show up in your body and on your face. When you feel better, you'll look better.

Right now, notice if any part of you feels uncomfortable. Make a simple adjustment to feel better. It's easy to do. That little adjustment can connect you with yourself in a loving way.

The more you touch, the more touched you will be.

You probably experience the world around you mostly through sight. You'll walk by hundreds of things today that you'll see but you won't touch.

As a child you were more tactile, touching everything you saw, holding it in your hands, and putting it in your mouth. As you grew up you were probably taught to suppress those tactile urges and keep your hands to yourself.

So now you'll walk by a tree covered in moss without knowing the feel of the nubby rough bark and soft green fuzz. You'll smile at the curly haired pooch without running your hands through its coat. You'll shop without feeling the weight and texture of the fabrics before you try clothes on.

If you reach out and touch life around you, you'll begin to accept and even appreciate your need for touch.

Touch yourself in loving ways.

I invite you to touch your thumb to the fingers on the same hand, very slowly. Close your eyes and explore the texture of your skin as you move your thumb around. Stroke lightly and feel how your skin responds. The slower you move, the more you'll feel. Do this for just a few moments with your eyes closed.

When you stop, notice the sensations, energy, and sense of life in your hand. You'll probably be aware of that hand for a while after you've stopped touching. The life was always inside you, but your touch brought it to your awareness.

You can enliven yourself any time with the touch of your own hand.

Run your fingers along a part of your own body that feels pleasurable; your mouth, your stomach, your feet or collarbone. Then do the same for body parts that rarely get loved; the back of your knees, the inside of your wrist, or the crease behind your ear. Do it slowly. Pay attention.

The parts that are most pleasurable for you will be different than mine, so explore your body and discover new pleasure points with your touch.

Discover yourself, and the world around you, through touch. It doesn't have to take long. Even one slow moment of focusing on sensory pleasure can alter your state of being, like a deep meditation.

It may seem glaringly obvious, but adding more touch to love making will increase your pleasure. Explore your partner's body through touch, discovering new areas that please you both. Your lips to her belly. The back of your hand to his neck. Try new ways to feel each other. Get to know each other more deeply through touch.

You can't give touch without getting touched back.

Hug your children, your folks, and the homeless person who needs it most. Visit seniors who are isolated and give them a hand massage. Groom neglected dogs in a shelter. Hold premature babies at hospitals when their parents can't be with them.

When I worked in a store that sold skin products, an elderly lady used to come in every few months to buy a tiny bottle of our foot lotion. Miss Cuthbertson was quick witted, with a sharp mind and frail body. Even though she just lived across the street from our shop, the trip for her was treacherous.

I started bringing the lotion to her, and this became a ritual for us. When I arrived at her cozy apartment she'd be sitting in a green lounge chair, with a big smile on her face. I'd drop my bags at the door, sit on the floor in front of her chair, and pour some lotion into my hands.

As I held her tiny feet and rubbed her delicate skin, she would tell me fascinating stories from her life. She'd been the only child of missionary parents and had become a missionary herself. She'd lived in more countries than I will probably ever see. She'd had great adventures and an enduring faith.

She'd outlived all of her close friends, and other than going to church, she didn't get out much. But she was one of the most content people I'd ever met, happy with her history, her choices, and her life.

She had a great sense of humor and always made me laugh.

After 8 or 10 hours of standing, serving other people, it was so relaxing to hold her feet and just get lost in her stories and her love.

Within a few years of meeting her, Miss Cuthbertson's health deteriorated and she was moved to a care facility. I went to visit her there a few times before she died. Though she didn't seem to recognize me, she let me rub her feet while she lay quietly in her bed.

As soon as I put my hands on her body I felt peaceful. I'm not sure if it was the peace in her infusing me through our touch, or just the peace within me rising up to my awareness. Even without her stories, or her welcoming smile, I was always deeply touched just to be with her, holding her feet.

Touch creates a connection when words fail.

I was working with Garth and Sue who were happy enough in their marriage, but they lacked the deep joyful connection that is possible. They often triggered each other in conversations and would retreat into their own wounds, living as distant but pleasant roommates rather than intimate partners, lovers, and friends. She often felt abandoned and he feared her disapproval.

In private, I gave Garth a new practice to try. "Touch Sue every day; just a brief, non-sexual touch. It can be anything you like, just keep it simple. You can touch the small of her back when you pass her in the kitchen. Hug her when you tell her you're going out. Rest your leg across hers when you're reading on the couch. Anything you want. Just once every day."

It takes courage to risk being vulnerable and try something new, especially in relationship where patterns are set. I would text Garth regular reminders because new habits take a while to form and it's easy to fall back into old ways.

A few months later, both of them reported separately that things were better between them. They were being kinder to each other. Garth admitted the changes were subtle, but the touch was enabling him to open up more and stay close. Sue didn't know what was different, but she was enjoying Garth's presence more.

That may not seem like much, but in long term relationships it's easy to feel stale and grow apart. The tenderness that began with one simple touch a day was a doorway to more intimacy, acceptance, and love.

Touch is a powerful and pleasurable way to bring more well-being, connection, and presence into your life. Explore the texture and temperature of food with your tongue, feel the air caress your nostrils, experience the cold rain on your face and the warm earth beneath your feet. Simply by touching and being touched you'll feel more alive.

Like diet, exercise, and meditation, you'll want to practice touch daily for best results. Over time you'll experience the cumulative benefits.

These following practices will wake up your body, fill your needs, and open you up to more touch, more pleasure, and more presence.

TOUCH

Practices

– Guided Meditation for Touch –

The following practices will all fit seamlessly into your day and bring the pleasure of touch into your life. They take no extra time.

You can also go to: www.debrajoy.me/practices for a guided meditation on touch. It's 6 minutes long.

– Be Touched –

When you notice the ways you're being held and supported you'll relax more into your body. What's touching you on the outside can awaken you to the life inside.

From the moment you wake up until you go to bed, notice all the ways in which life is touching you.

- The sheets against your body, the temperature of the shower water, your clothes as you put them on, the fork in your hand, the keyboard under your fingers.

Notice how each touch makes you feel, both physically and emotionally.

Make any adjustments you'd like, once you've noticed how you feel.

Pick a trigger that will remind you to pay attention. Such as:

- Focus on what's touching you the moment you wake.
- Feel how you're being touched whenever you eat.
- Notice what's touching you every time your phone rings.

All day long life is caressing you and holding you. Often you're so busy in your mind, perhaps even dreaming about the touch you want, that you miss the ways life is touching you already.

– TOUCH LIFE –

Increasing your physical contact with life will enrich your experience in deep and simple ways. Life is always offering you textures, temperatures, movement, and stillness to explore.

 Let your eyes look around.

 Notice what attracts or interests you most.

 Touch it.

 You can start with your hands, but use other parts of your body whenever possible. Vary speeds and pressure and notice the changes in how it feels to you.

As you interact with your world through touch you'll become present. You'll experience your world and yourself in a deeper way.

– CREATE A TOUCH RITUAL –

Ritual has the power to turn ordinary events into sacred acts. These simple rituals don't require any extra time. They're just offering you an opportunity to become present to pleasure in these moments throughout your day.

 Choose a moment in your day for touch.

 Treat it as a ritual.

 It can include:

- Washing your face in the morning as an act of self love. Feel the connection between your fingers and face.

- Applying lotion on your body before you go to bed. Feel your body relax as you prepare to sleep.

- Shaving, brushing your hair, and soaping your body can all become rituals of touch.

 Pay attention to the sensations under your skin as you practice these touch rituals.

When you focus on the sensations in your body as you touch yourself, it can feel as if time is suspended. You slow the moment down, without taking more time. This can calm your system and help you feel less busy, more in control.

– TOUCH OTHERS –

Find simple ways to give more touch to the beings you love.

- Hug.
- Hold hands.
- Scratch backs.
- Rub feet.
- Give a massage.
- Brush their hair or fur.

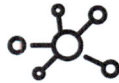

Touch acquaintances and friends to create more connection.

- Shake hands.
- High five.
- Give pats on the back.

Notice how you feel when you touch.

Let yourself be touched in simple ways.

Animals and humans can read the energy of another's touch. They may feel your support, encouragement, and love in a more direct way than words could convey. If you pay attention as you're touching, you'll fill yourself up with connection as well.

– Your Practice –

What:

_____

Name this practice

Why:

_____

_____

What do you expect to gain from this practice?
Knowing why you're doing it will help keep you motivated.

Break your practice down into very simple steps.

1. _____

   _____

2. _____

   _____

3. _____

   _____

4. _____

   _____

Trigger:

_____

When developing a new habit it's best to do it every day, at the same time if possible, and it's important to have something that reminds you, or triggers you to do it.

What will trigger you to do this practice?

- NOTES -

TASTE

"TASTE EVERY FRUIT OF EVERY TREE IN THE GARDEN AT LEAST ONCE. IT IS AN INSULT TO CREATION NOT TO EXPERIENCE IT FULLY."

– STEPHEN FRY

I invite you right now to close your eyes and think about eating your favorite food.

If you did it, just in that moment of imagining good food, your body prepared for it. Your mouth probably became moist, filling with digestive juices. You may notice that your mouth still feels juicy.

Let's say you imagined baked apples. You could probably smell the cinnamon before you took a bite. You could feel the wrinkly soft skin touching your lips, the flesh of apples sliding on your tongue, the hard crunch of walnuts and gush of plump raisins popping between your teeth. You may sense the heat warming you from inside.

Eating is a sensuous act.

It can be as delightful and mysterious as making love if you surrender fully to the sensations. At some point you've cried "Oh My God" at a taste so divine it felt sacred and holy. Or moaned as a delicious flavor seeped beyond your mouth and filled your body.

You're meant to enjoy your food.

Your mouth is a dark, moist cave of pleasurable potential. At the entrance to this cavern of delight are your sensitive lips; thin-membraned, and packed with nerve endings. Within it, your strong teeth crush food, expressing the flavors hidden inside and preparing it for digestion. From your fleshy cheeks and smooth palate, to your soft, sinuous tongue, your mouth is covered in thousands of taste buds.

It's the ideal environment for sensuous living. And it's all within you. Several times a day you can easily indulge in the textures, temperatures, and tastes of food.

Eating is a pleasurable invitation to presence.

Meditation is one of the proven ways to experience more peace, acceptance, and compassion.[16] Meditation is simply the practice of becoming present by giving your mind an anchor to focus on. The smaller the area of focus, the greater your focus will be.

Let the sensations in your mouth be your anchor.

By focusing your attention in your mouth as you eat, your mind drops the chatter, (the never-ending list of things to do, worries, negative self talk, and planning), which is the cause of most of your stress.

Thoughts are constantly bouncing between the past and future. That's just what thoughts do. Rather than try to control your thinking, you can become completely present by simply focusing on the sensations of taste.

Confucius said, "Everyone eats and drinks, but few appreciate taste."

What you taste is a combination of the smell, texture and temperature of your food. Over 70% of flavor comes from the smell. That's why food loses its taste when you have a cold. The mucus in your nasal passages blocks the odor molecules of your food from reaching the olfactory receptor cells in your brain.[17]

To fully indulge in the sensuous meditation of eating, take time to smell your food.

Smell to savor what you eat. Slowly inhale the aroma of food and notice how you feel. You'll become much more satisfied with food if you let yourself smell it. This takes practice. It's a habit for most of us to quickly gobble our meals without involving all of our senses.

When you take a bite, fully indulge in the experience.

You can melt into the satisfaction of silky smooth chocolate on your tongue, awaken to the spicy roughness of chorizo against your palate, or be refreshed by the sweet sharpness of a crisp piece of apple inside your cheeks.

If you already meditate, this is a delicious way to bring more meditative moments into your life. If you aren't meditating, this is a tasty way to experience the pleasure of presence several times a day.

The benefits of meditation last long beyond your last bite.

When practiced regularly, meditation helps you control impulses and cravings.[18] It can improve your sleep and helps you handle stress better, which moves your body out of fat-storage mode.[19] So it may also be that the more you enjoy your food, the easier it will be to maintain a healthy weight.

When you fill up with pleasure you're not as hungry.

You may be worried that if you slow down to really taste your food it will take too long. You're already rushed to finish your meals.

You'll see in the practice portion of this chapter that I invite you to start by meditating on just the first bite. Taking one slow luxurious bite won't slow you down, but it will fill you up.

Guided by pleasure, you'll meditate on more and more bites. You'll discover that the feeling of being satiated comes much sooner when you immerse yourself in the sensations of each bite.

You'll likely find yourself eating less and enjoying it more. By focusing on your food while you eat it, you'll stop obsessing about food between meals.

Fully indulging in your food helps you feel better in your body and more satisfied in your life.

When I lead retreats, I choose places where women can get in touch with their authentic nature in a wild environment. Food is a big part of the experience. Eating delicious, organic, local foods without distraction is a chance to connect with life intimately several times a day. I use these opportunities for each participant to connect with her body's wisdom through pleasure.

As we eat our breakfast outdoors, with our feet on the earth, we taste the delicate seasoning of scrambled eggs, roll the sweet, sticky flesh of fried plantains over our tongues, and swallow the slick juices of watermelon, papaya, and guanabana. We are not rushed. It's a wonderful way to start the day.

At least once during the week we'll eat an entire meal blindfolded. We sit around the table as we normally would. Being unable to see changes how we eat and how we interact. We slow down even more. We are quieter than usual, and when we speak, it is mostly about our experience in the moment.

I instruct the women not to take the blindfolds off until they feel completely satisfied. When they remove them, most are shocked to see a good portion of their meal untouched, even though they feel full.

You've probably heard the expression that your eyes are bigger than your stomach. As long as you see food on your plate, you'll probably keep eating, until you become stuffed. By blocking sight you rely on other senses. By slowing down, you feel the sensations in your body and know when you've had enough.

By smelling, tasting, and feeling food, you'll be satiated with pleasure long before you feel full. And pleasure fills you up for a long time.

Unfortunately, food can also be a source of stress.

Lots of people struggle with food. I certainly have. Many times eating has nothing to do with hunger. You may eat for many reasons: to treat yourself, feel a connection, or fill a void. You can use food to distract yourself from things you don't want to face, or numb the emotions you don't want to feel; boredom, frustration, sadness, even joy.

You may be thinking "I've gobbled pretzels out of boredom, and I've drowned my sorrows in a pint of Ben and Jerry's, but why would I avoid joy??" As surprising as it seems it's not just the bad feelings that make us uncomfortable. Some good feelings are at times too much to handle.

If you haven't learned to breathe and ground to enable big feelings to move through you, even the "good ones" can make you run for the fridge.

If you fill yourself with food to numb your feelings, you miss an opportunity to fully experience life. The feelings that are trying to move through you stay trapped inside. You end up feeling weighed down from holding in emotions and eating food your body didn't want.

If your life is busy you may rush while you eat and miss many of the pleasures food offers. You multi-task while eating rather than focusing on food's delights. You notice the first bite if you're lucky, and then you're probably distracted until you feel full.

It's easy to overeat this way. Since you're hard-wired for pleasure you keep consuming, hoping to be satisfied. Yet as long as you eat without paying attention, the pleasure of taste eludes you.

You can also separate yourself from the joy of eating by worrying about fat content, calories, or pesticide use.

Your body responds to these negative thoughts by producing extra stress hormones. These hormones interfere with your body's ability to digest your food, and actually make you hold onto fat longer than you normally would.[20] Sadly, just worrying about fat can make you fatter.

When you allow yourself to indulge in tastes, you experience the physical sensations that make you feel content, and the craving for more subsides.

Perhaps you deprive yourself of food, feeling unworthy of the pleasure and nourishment food can bring, even ashamed of the flesh it can add to your bones. In this case food becomes a form of punishment and a cause for shame.

Whether you're comforting or depriving, food can't fix your emotional problems. It won't satisfy your natural need for love, acceptance, and connection. But paying attention to taste can connect you back to your self, and bring you not just pleasure, but peace.

Your cravings are your body's wisdom speaking to you.

Your taste can really support your health. When you crave something specific it's usually because your body needs the particular nutrients from that food. Your cells know what they need to be healthy, and they send messages to your brain to seek it out. Unless you have a food allergy or addiction your body will guide you to what it needs.

Since your body's requirements are constantly in flux, your taste preferences will change accordingly. If you pay attention to your body's requests and use these simple practices to connect with your food, you'll feed yourself what you really need and be richly rewarded.

A while back, my nutritionist asked if I would be willing to eat raw oysters as a way to build up zinc in my body. Absolutely. I love oysters. I began eating them regularly. Then one day I noticed I didn't want them at all. My body was saying NO. But since I thought I was "supposed" to eat them, I bought them anyway. They tasted terrible.

I told my nutritionist what happened and she said that's exactly what should happen. When your body has sufficient zinc, the taste changes. It was my body's way of saying I'd had enough. If I'd trusted that my body knew best when it was saying NO, I would have given my body the break from zinc that I needed.

The genius of our bodies continues to amaze me, and I only know a fraction of its deep wisdom.

To improve my digestion I learned to chew my food more. I still have lots of room for improvement, as I'm a habitually fast eater. Feeling my feet on the ground and breathing deeply while I eat slows me down. When I'm slower I remember to chew.

I invite you to do the same. Chew until solids become liquids. This will aid your digestion, but don't chew just for that. Explore the changing textures and tastes with every bite you take. Lose yourself in the pleasure of eating.

By listening to my body rather than overriding it, I've benefited from its wisdom. At times I've felt a yearning deep in my bones for the earthy taste of beef broth, while my mouth craved the bright tart juices of a fresh orange. The two desires seemed at odds with each other until I learned that collagen, which is in broth, is better absorbed by the body with vitamin C, which is in the oranges. Somehow my body knew what I needed it before my mind could figure out why.

Even though my diet isn't completely pure, I trust that my body knows what it needs f I will just listen to it. That gives me great peace. I try to tune out all the contradictory messages telling me how I should eat, and listen to my body by feeling what I truly desire. My connection with food has become intimate and personal.

Addiction speaks a different language.

You can't trust your cravings, or give yourself over to pleasure, if you're dealing with addiction. It muddles the clear messages from your body and overrides your inner wisdom.

People often confuse pleasure with addiction. The contrast is subtle but profound.

Pleasure nourishes you.

It feels good when you're indulging in it and it leaves you feeling good about yourself afterwards. People use words like expansive, strong, relaxed, joyful, and peaceful to describe themselves after indulging in pleasures. Pleasure connects you to yourself, and beyond yourself to all of life.

Addiction depletes you.

An addictive habit may feel good when you're indulging in it. You can feel high, euphoric even, but it will leave you with mixed emotions. You may feel stuffed, but longing for more. When the high of addiction wears off people say they feel small, contracted, ashamed, guilty, resentful, and unworthy. Yet the craving for more soon returns.

If you can't control cravings it's important to know that it's not a sign of weakness.

Addiction changes your brain.

It alters the reward center of your brain. This part of your brain lights up when dopamine neurotransmitters link up with the dopamine receptors, and makes you feel good.

With an addiction, the brain becomes overwhelmed and responds by producing less dopamine. This means that over time the same amount of (whatever you're addicted to) provides less pleasure. But the memory of the pleasure remains, so you crave more and more, trying to get that high you once felt.[21]

Addiction impairs the executive function of your brain, which enables you to organize, strategize, be mindful, patient, and control your impulses.[22] That explains why you may not be able to stop yourself from eating more candies or potato chips than you want. It's no wonder you feel helpless when it comes to addictive behaviors.

Unaware of the nourishment you really need, you consume compulsively, only to be racked with shame afterwards, feeling stuffed but emotionally empty and longing for more.

The good news is that all of this is changeable. Your brain is highly adaptable.

Treat your body right and it will right itself.

Sugar is more addictive than cocaine, but it's a lot easier to get.[23] Even if you don't add sugar to your diet, it's hiding in processed foods. It's not just in those cookies, pies, and sodas. It's in your pretzels, cereals, and pasta sauce. You may be feeding a sugar addiction, without even realizing it.

If you eat the typical North American diet you're saturating your body with sugar unknowingly. As well as robbing you of your health, it deadens your ability to taste the delicate sweetness that occurs naturally in foods.

Many years ago I was very ill with digestive pain and undiagnosed celiac disease. I had to go on a strict diet for several years. I sadly gave up my vegetarian lifestyle. I stopped eating all grains, starchy vegetables, dairy, fruits, honey and sugar of any kinds.

My diet has since expanded, and I can eat fruit again. One day I picked up a ripe slice of peach at a farmer's market. I took a small bite. The jewel-toned flesh released its sacred juices between my teeth and gushed over my tongue. I closed my eyes for just a moment and was taken on a juicy journey deep into my own sensations.

I'd always loved peaches, but this first taste after kicking my sugar habit, was more delicious than any I could remember. I was completely satisfied by just one bite, and can feel the pleasure of that moment again as I write about it now.

Longing is a desire for what you don't have.

When you allow yourself to fill up with tastes, the desire for more subsides.

I don't know if it's because I'm half Irish, but I've never met a potato I didn't like. Potato chips were my downfall. I would practically inhale them, while feeling guilty and judging myself.

Then one day I decided to slow down. I'd enjoy the crisp crunch as I bit down. Feel the salty roughness on my tongue. I indulged in the texture and flavor of each chip. I breathed deeply while I ate.

Over time something happened. I was experiencing them more but enjoying them less. What was once pleasurable was now irritating my palate. The cravings dissolved. It's rare now that I eat potato chips.

When I do eat them, I realize that I'm usually just tired and wanting a hit of energy. I haven't eaten enough protein or fat, or gotten enough rest. Though sleep or nutritious food is really what I need, when I'm too lazy to give myself either, I still sometimes find myself reaching for the chips as a cheap fix. Even then I give them my attention and enjoy them the best I can.

Breathing deeply throughout the day, and while you eat, can help you curb cravings. Deep breathing slows your breath down, making you feel calm, in control, and capable of handling cravings or challenges."[24]

Change your relationship with food and your life will change.

When I'm working with clients who are having trouble focusing, sticking to their direction, or getting clear on their own desires, I will often ask about their food.

Diane is a client whose life really changed by shifting her focus from food as reward and punishment, to treating food as a source of pleasure and nourishment.

Diane was divorced and living in New York City. She loved her high-powered corporate job, even though it was stressful. She was healthy enough, but she felt like she was dragging her ass through the day, living on caffeine, and collapsing on the couch most evenings after work.

She hired me as an executive coach while in the middle of a big transition in her work. We were working on the specifics of her career, when I said, "Tell me about your relationship to food." She broke down in tears.

For the past few years she'd been starting her day with carbs and caffeine to get going. She'd eat a decent lunch and sometimes a pretty balanced dinner. Then, for having worked so hard, she'd treat herself with alcohol, sweets, and snacks. She didn't want to think about the mid-day sodas and lattes she'd slurped for energy, how many gourmet cupcakes she'd picked up on her way home, or the bags of pretzels that had kept her company on the couch while she fell asleep watching movies.

She felt weak when it came to food, and that made her feel badly about herself. Diane was smart, funny, and attractive, but she didn't feel good in her own body.

Since Diane was facing new challenges and exceptional opportunities in her career, I asked if she would do something radical and go on a sugar detox for a month while I continued coaching her. I felt it would give her some clarity, since her current way of eating was putting her in a fructose fog.

Studies show that excess sugar impairs cognitive abilities and slows synaptic activity in the brain.[25] With the pressure of the new position and the decisions she was going to face, I thought that freedom from sugar would help her think clearly.

Diane was frightened, which wasn't surprising. She was going to want her comforts more than ever during this leap in her career. She was about to step into the spotlight with more pressure on her, and the idea of adding this level of stress freaked her out. I invited all of her resistance into our sessions, and we discussed each valid complaint.

In the end she trusted me to support her, and I promised she could quit any time. I used a 21-day program that was designed by a colleague of mine. It's nutritious, safe, and super effective. (Go to www.debrajoy.me/resources.)

Breaking the sugar habit was tough at first. Without rewarding, punishing, and numbing herself with food, she had to feel her emotions, including her fear, excitement, and pride. I was able to provide support in those areas, which made the detox easier.

She stuck with the program beyond the 21 days because she liked the changes she was experiencing. She was sleeping better, feeling more energetic, and by her fifth week she was jumping off the subway early and walking part of the way home. On the weekends she started hiking with her girlfriends.

I continued working with Diane for over a year. She incorporated more food into her life, one item at a time, noticing how each affected her body and mind. During that time she developed more self-care practices, and her self-worth soared. It wasn't a linear process, and not without its setbacks, but her progress was remarkable.

Her decision-making skills sharpened as she learned to listen to her own wisdom, which was made easier without the confusion of "sugar brain" getting in the way.

With this newfound clarity, Diane had some powerful realizations. Ever since her divorce she'd been dating men who treated her like trash, and she let them. She was ashamed of her personal life. She realized that her addiction to these men was mirroring her addiction to sugar. The men, like sweets, looked exciting at first, suggesting promises of a thrilling romance. But just like cupcakes, they left her feeling empty and longing for more.

She was the one with the power to choose, and the longer Diane stayed off sugar the more she chose to love herself in different areas of life.

She also realized that her exciting new position wasn't really what she wanted. Though its high profile fed her ego and was the next logical step in her corporate climb, it gave her less connection with clients, which had been the part of her work she loved most.

After 18 months of living sugar free, Diane made a bold move at the office and created a new position that enabled her to work directly with colleagues and clients in a way that fed her soul. She also met and married a man who cherishes her.

Once she began loving and treating herself well, life seemed to respond in kind.

Diane's soul had been hungry for a long time. In the confusion of addiction she'd misread those hunger pains and fed them with junk, leaving her feeling stuffed but empty. By removing the sugar she was able to hear the truth of her hunger and feed herself with the nourishment she really needed.

Not everyone has an addiction to sugar, so this may not apply to you.

If cravings are robbing you of the pleasure of indulging in food, then you might benefit from a sugar detox. Like many of my clients, you may discover a whole new vitality and clarity as your brain heals itself from addiction.

I recommend getting as much support as possible when doing any detox program. (Go to www.debrajoy.me/resources for the Resource Guide).

Food allergies and sensitivities can disrupt your ability to sense what your body needs and enjoy food. Getting professional support for your digestion can be a loving act of self care. Over the years I've worked with a highly skilled Nutritional Therapy Practitioner to help me. (Go to www.debrajoy.me/resources for the Resource Guide)

Since you're already eating, I invite you to fully indulge. Treat a mouthful as a meditation by focusing on the pleasure. It's a simple way to connect with your body in loving ways several times a day. Slowing down to feel the sensations can be a delicious and direct path to your true self.

TASTE

PRACTICES

– Guided Taste Meditation –

Most of the practices in this chapter take no extra time and will fit seamlessly into your life. To get the most out of those practices you will benefit from following this 5 minute guided meditation to experience the pleasure of food.

For this meditation you will need two things: a piece of fruit and privacy.

You may be tempted to just listen to the meditation without the fruit, or without actually doing the meditation. There's a big difference between thinking you understand something because you've heard or read it and actually experiencing it. Ask any woman who's given birth.

You'll only truly understand this practice by experiencing it for yourself. You may feel resistant to doing the guided practice because whether you're aware of it or not it feels safer to just listen to it. Change can be scary, even if it's change that you want.

- Get a piece of fruit and set aside 5 minutes of time.

- Go to: www.debrajoy.me/practices and I will guide you through a mediation on taste.

– Fill Yourself With Aromas –

You can do this practice with things you're about to eat, or things you aren't going to eat. I have celiac, so I don't eat bread, but I still indulge in the aroma, and feel the homey pleasure through my whole body.

 Close your eyes and inhale the scent of your food.

 Move the food back and forth under your nose and breathe deeply.

 Notice the complexity or simplicity of the aroma.

 Feel the sensations in your body as you experience the smell.

Taking time to smell before you eat will help prepare your body for digestion. And you'll definitely get more pleasure from your food.

– Make Your First Bite a Meditation –

During the first bite of each meal you eat, use these aspects of the guided meditation to connect with your food and yourself in a pleasurable way.

 See and smell: Be curious and explore the shapes, variety of colors and smells of your food, as if for the very first time.

 Taste: Notice the temperature, textures and taste changing as you slowly chew your food. Chew until it is dissolved.

 Connect: Think of all that went into growing this food and getting it to you. You may even give thanks for everything and everyone involved.

 Pause: Notice how you feel before you take another bite.

Gratitude improves all areas of your life from your physical and mental health to your self esteem and relationships. Step 3 is an important part of this quick and simple meditation.

– Close Your Eyes –

This simple one bite practice will heighten your experience in the moment, and make you more present.

 Close your eyes for just one bite. Bring your attention to the feelings in your mouth.

 Explore how the sensations of taste change as you chew until your food dissolves.

 Ground and breathe. Feel where your body connects to the ground or a chair and let yourself relax down into those places. Breathe through your nose.

 Pause after you swallow. Just notice how you feel.

It's easy to slip this practice into one bite of anything you're eating. You'll be surprised how much more you experience when you simply close your eyes. And of course you can continue with your eyes closed for as many bites as you like. Which leads to our next practice...

– EAT A MEAL BLINDFOLDED –

This practice takes a little more preparation and is best done in a private setting. It can be a transformative practice to do on your own, and particularly fun to do with someone else. (You will each need a blindfold for this practice)

 Prepare. Before you tie on your blindfold, put your food and drink where you can find it without knocking anything over. To make it easier you can eat your meal with your hands.

 Put on your blindfold. Get comfortable. Feel your feet on the floor and your bum in the chair. Let your body drop down and rest into the places where it is being supported. Take a few slow, easy breaths.

 Notice and share. Explore the different taste sensations and feelings you experience by limiting your senses. Share your experience if you're eating with others.

 Finish when you're satisfied. Remove your blindfold when you feel done. You may be surprised to see that there's food left on your plate even though you feel satiated.

Seeing food on your plate will often trigger you to eat more, even though you're not hungry. A way to overcome that is to immediately dump what's left into the compost, or put it in the fridge for later. Trust that you are done with it for now.

Most of us eat more than we really want because we see it in front of us. The mind overrides the body's wisdom, wanting to eat all that it sees, sometimes longing for even more. The ego is never satisfied.

There's also a biological reason for eating all that you see. In your ancestors' hunting and gathering days there would have been long stretches without food. So you're designed to eat as much as possible when food is available. The only problem is that now food is always available. When you connect with your senses, you're satisfied with less because you tasted it, you experienced it, and you ate slower, so your body had time to know when it was full.

Eating in this way, you become present to the delights of food and the natural pleasures of eating. You discover a new sense of how much is enough. It may take time to trust this new version of "full." Removing the leftover food immediately will support this learning curve.

Do It Alone

Doing this alone on a regular basis is a powerful way to feel and honor what your body wants and needs. It can change your relationship with food from punishment and shame to nourishment and pleasure. You'll naturally eat the right amount of the food when you stop overriding your body's wisdom. You'll enjoy eating. Your relationship to food and your body will transform.

Enhance Your Romance

You can also use this practice to heighten your senses with a partner. While the practice pulls your attention inward, you can share the sensations you're feeling as you're experiencing them.

It's a great way to be present with someone you love and share your inner world in a way that is both safe an intimate. This can spil over into other aspects of your private life and enhance your intimate connection.

Feed Your Family

This practice is also a fun way to eat with your kids. Let them be explorers, discovering the tastes, textures, and sensations of food. Invite them to inhale aromas and eat with their hands. Encourage them to share their experiences.

If they describe what they taste without labeling it as "gross" or "yummy," they can begin to decipher new tastes and expand their palate. With permission to eat only what they want, they learn to trust their bodies.

– Your Practice –

WHAT:

_____

Name this practice

WHY:

_____

_____

What do you expect to gain from this practice?
Knowing why you're doing it will help keep you motivated.

BREAK YOUR PRACTICE DOWN INTO VERY SIMPLE STEPS.

1. _____

    _____

2. _____

    _____

3. _____

    _____

4. _____

    _____

TRIGGER:

_____

When developing a new habit it's best to do it every day, at the same time if possible, and it's
important to have something that reminds you, or triggers you to do it.

What will trigger you to do this practice?

- NOTES -

SLEEP

"SLEEP IS THE BEST MEDITATION"

- THE DALAI LAMA

You know the soothing feeling of crawling between crisp clean sheets, or snuggling into a warm sleeping bag, on a cool night, under a sky full of stars.

There's a deliciousness that overtakes you when you let your body and mind surrender. Your thoughts dissolve and you drift off to sleep. You leave the linear world of time and space, problems and goals, success and disappointments, and are transported to the mysterious realm of healing and restoration.

Sleeping does for you what powering down does for your computer.

It gives you a reboot.

After a good sleep it's easier to tap into the life force within you, and let your light shine. Whether your light emanates from the brilliance of your mind, the strength and grace of your body, or the love in your heart, it shines brighter after a good sleep, and it's dimmed when you're tired.

Sleep feels luxurious but it's no luxury. It's as important to your body as food or water. It's so vital to wellbeing that sleep deprivation is a tactic often used in torture.

And yet many of us... Resist it. Skip it. Fear it and resent it.

Sometimes we long for it and still we deprive ourselves of it, by staying up too late, waking up too early, and powering through the day on stimulants and adrenaline. Long term - we're torturing ourselves. How very undelicious.

Sleep is the secret ingredient that will make every part of your life better.

It will improve your relationships.

When you haven't slept you're more likely to be irritable and tense, even with people you love. This can create unnecessary friction.

After a good sleep you're more relaxed and at ease. You're kinder to your kids and partner. It's easier to be understanding and compassionate. You're more cheerful and more likely to laugh, even at yourself. All of this buoys your relationships.

If it's been so long since you slept well that you don't remember what it's like to be this awesome with the people you love, just look at your kids. You know they're better humans when they've slept.

You'll be more successful at work and school.

When you've slept well you're more alert and productive, better able to focus. It fuels your brain so you're more creative and better at problem solving. During sleep your brain sorts through all your experiences of the day and consolidates it into memories. It prioritizes what's important to keep, and what can be discarded. Sleep deprivation inhibits this.[35]

So if you're studying or preparing a presentation for work, you'll have better recall the next day if you get a good sleep than if you stay up too late working on it.

My client Barb wrote to me after taking my advice to get more sleep, "I had no idea how much I could accomplish by doing less and sleeping more. It's now the secret ingredient of my success".

Who said anything about sex?

I did, just now. While sleep isn't a very seductive topic, it nourishes your flow of sexual chi and can do wonders for your sex life. There's nothing sexy about dragging your ass through the day, no matter how good your butt looks in those jeans.

When was the last time you felt exhausted and aroused at the same time?

See what I mean. When you indulge in sleep, you fuel your brain and body for more excitement and connection. So first go to bed. Get some sleep. Lots of it. Then go to bed and indulge in other pleasures.

Sleep is sacred.

When you sleep, your breathing regulates, and your brain patterns become more synchronous and coordinated.

Sounds an awful lot like meditation, doesn't it?

If you're a meditator, you know that peace probably didn't come the first time you sat down and tried to focus. And many times you sit to meditate your mind is still busy.

But with years of practice you've changed your brain. People who meditate regularly experience more peace, clarity and compassion.

The first few times I tried to meditate I thought it was an impossible task. But over the years, the practice has changed my life, giving me peace in challenging times, calming my busy mind, and enabling me to hear my own inner guidance. I've become kinder to myself.

Your thoughts are your biggest source of stress. Not what's happening in your life, but your thoughts about it. Your mind is busy all day thinking, planning, and often worrying.

With the thousands of thoughts your mind thinks automatically, most of them on repeat, it can be a challenge to hear your own divine wisdom through all the noise. That wisdom could calm your worries, ease your stress, and give you guidance.

Sleep can be a portal to that wise source inside you.

In the Rapid Eye Movement, (REM), stage of sleep, you process issues from the day access messages, guidance and even premonitions, through your dreams. Your brain sorts through what's important and what's not, and builds new connections. It's not uncommon to wake with the solution to an issue, an inspired new idea, or a fresh optimistic perspective.

If you stay up at night working on a problem, you might feel the weight of it grow and smother you in the darkness. The harder it presses down on you, the harder you push yourself to solve it. When you're wrestling with a problem you just can't solve, it's often a good idea to "sleep on it."

Even if you don't wake with a clear answer to your problem, the new connections your brain made during a night's sleep will enable you to handle challenges and come up with solutions more easily.

Dreaming is a powerful part of sleep.

Sometimes solutions will come to you in dreams, in ways you hadn't even imagined.

Several years ago I decided to lead my first women's retreat. For several days I woke each morning with an entire day's plan mapped out for me in my sleep. All I had to do was write down what I remembered from my dreams. These processes that became the bulk of the retreat, were "downloaded" to me while I slept. Designing a retreat that way was so easy that it felt like cheating.

What happened to me might not be something you've experienced, but dreams are an important and powerful part of sleep.

Carl Jung said that dreams promote the most important developmental process of your life; uniting consciousness with the unconscious, leading to the actualization of your whole being.[36]

When you surrender to sleep, you let go of your firmly held ideas and beliefs that make up your identity, the very constructs that keep you from realizing your true self.

Sleep may be the simplest path to awakening. And you're just not getting enough.

Lack of sleep wreaks havoc on your body.

If you've got a car you know how important regular maintenance is. If you skip it you'll probably deal with bigger repair problems later on.

A friend and I were recently driving from LA to Joshua Tree. Her car was making a weird noise in the back. She'd been driving it for years without doing maintenance on it. It had seemed fine, until now.

When we returned to the city, she took it to a mechanic who said the brake pads had worn down. That would have been easy and cheap to fix if we'd caught it earlier, but since they hadn't been replaced quickly enough, the wear and tear had damaged the rotors. Those were more expensive to replace. If we'd waited any longer to repair the damaged rotors we could have experienced brake failure, putting ourselves, and others, at great risk.

Treat your body as if it's the only vehicle you'll ever have. Whether your favorite car is a Lamborghini, Ferrari, or Tesla, know that your body is more complex, precise and exquisite than the finest cars in the world.

Your body needs regular maintenance and repairs to avoid accidents and illness, even if it seems to be running fine. During sleep you regenerate and repair body tissue, boost your moods, and improve brain function. While it can be inconvenient to have your car in the shop for maintenance, it can be deadly to avoid it.

If you continually skimp on the repairs to your body that sleep provides, your physical and mental performance will suffer, and eventually you'll become sick.

Lack of sleep can pack on the pounds.

Many of us have been overriding our body's sleep signals for so long that we've stopped recognizing the signs. We confuse fatigue with hunger, and overeat for energy rather than getting the nourishment from rest that we really need.

Not getting enough sleep messes with your hormones.

Your body produces more ghrelin, the hormone that tells you you're hungry, and less leptin, the hormone that tells you when you're full.

As a result you overeat. Your stress hormone, cortisol, increases. That not only depresses your immune system and metabolism, it also causes your body to hold onto more fat.[37]

My client, Gail, was pretty overwhelmed with her executive role, her responsibilities at home, and finding time for herself. In her late forties, she was disgusted with the muffin top she'd gained. Even though she worked out regularly, she just couldn't lose it. Her doctor told her it was normal for menopausal women to have extra fat around the middle, but that didn't make her any happier.

She thought the only way to combat her belly was to work harder, but the harder she pushed herself, the more she felt at odds with her own body. And the muffin didn't budge. She thought about hiring a personal trainer and getting up earlier a few more days a week.

While I'm all for personal trainers, and getting lots of movement in life, I could tell the idea of adding one more thing to Gail's week was stressing her out before she even did it.

Gail wasn't getting enough sleep.

Once the kids were in bed she'd relax by flopping on the couch and scroll social media sites or watch television. Most nights she could feel how exhausted she was, but couldn't pull herself away. Sometimes she'd stay up until 1:00am because it was the only chance she had to be alone. The mornings she worked out she woke at 6:30am. Waking up early more mornings would have put her body under even more stress.

I invited Gail to try something new before adding more early morning workouts. I asked what her ideal sleep time would be, not what she wanted, but what she knew to be true. She didn't have to think about it. It was 10:00pm. She could feel it. I asked her if she'd be willing to make a commitment to go to bed by 10:00pm every single night (weekends included) for a week, as an experiment.

Even though she was exhausted, it was harder than you might think.

Gail had to work backwards from 10:00pm and plan out her evenings to be ready for bed on time. She had to set reminders for herself, to overcome her habits that led to staying up late. With some support, she got organized and began a week later. She set an alarm to ring every night at 9:30 to shut down electronics and get ready for bed.

She struggled at first. Sleep didn't come easily. Some nights she felt guilty for going to bed so early. Other times she felt like a child being punished, and she was pissed at me.

After a few weeks she had more energy.

After a month of going to bed early she felt better in her clothes.

She doesn't own a scale, so she didn't know if she'd lost weight, but she felt better. She realized she wasn't snacking as much, and her sugar cravings had eased. Once she was rested, she hired a personal trainer, and felt great about it. It was no longer one more way to beat her body into submission. It was something she wanted to do.

When you're exhausted, working harder is rarely the solution. Sleep usually is.

Lack of sleep messes with your mind.

Sleepy people have impaired judgment.

They're more likely to have accidents, make mistakes, and bad decisions. Yet we've got cities full of sleep deprived people driving cars, flying planes, writing exams, performing surgeries, running countries, and raising children. It seems the world would be better off if we'd all get more sleep.

Lack of sleep leads to trouble concentrating, difficulties reading and speaking, and in extreme cases it can cause hallucinations. That's why you struggle more in work, school and your personal life, when you don't get enough sleep for long periods of time.

Chronic lack of sleep can make you irritable, anxious, and even paranoid.

Simple problems will overwhelm you. You'll find yourself obsessing about money issues, relationship troubles, and situations at work, until they become monsters in the closet that won't let you rest.

We've all seen it before: a young child thrashing on the floor, crying and screaming, snot bubbling out of his nose. He's inconsolable, no matter what his parents try. It looks as if the kid's in terrible pain, being tortured even. But most often the parents will tell you, "He's just tired." When kids need sleep they can easily become overwhelmed by the feelings surging through their little bodies, like volcanoes erupting. They can act like monsters. But it's not that the little kid is being a problem. He's having a problem.

If you're a parent, you probably guard your child's sleep. You develop soothing rituals for bedtime, and make sure they get their naps. You do this not just to avoid tantrums, but as an act of love. You know they need sleep for their bodies and brains to grow and heal. They'll feel better when they wake up. They'll be happier, better able to the handle inevitable changes, and have more fun playing with others.

Sleep reduces stress.

You never outgrow your need for sleep, but without someone to guard it for you, it's unlikely you're getting as much as you need.

We deprive ourselves all the time, in favor of watching tv, scrolling social media, and working late into the night. No wonder highways, shopping centers, and relationships are full of tired people having accidents and arguments.

We're a society full of adults on the verge of tantrums from lack of sleep.

Even if you aren't raging and acting out like a child having a tantrum, that same irritable, tense, short-fused rush builds inside you when you're chronically tired. It takes a lot of your energy to hold it all in. You may get easily overwhelmed, feel weepy for no reason, blow up at your kids when they leave their socks on the floor, or snap at your mate when she asks a question.

When your body is tense and tired, you feel bad about yourself.

This can be the beginning of a vicious downward spiral. It's not that you're a bad parent, should be working harder, or need couples' counseling. You just need more sleep.

Jim Loehr, a leading sports psychologist, who trains people how to handle physical, mental and emotional stress for peak performance says "It's important to understand that only rarely does the volume of stress defeat us; far more often the agent of defeat is insufficient capacity for recovery after the stress."   Great stress simply requires great recovery.

The more stress you've got, the more rest you need. It's how your body, brain and moods recover. Sleeping more doesn't mean you're lazy. It means you're taking care of yourself.

Tim Ferriss, author of The Four Hour Workweek, says, "Being busy is a form of laziness."[39]

If you don't spend time discovering what's really important to you, and make choices that support what matters most, you'll stay busy. It's not a lack of hours in the day that's the problem. It's that you haven't been willing to make the tough choices.

To be able to say yes to the things that matter most, you're going to have to say no to the things that don't.

For most of us, saying yes to more sleep is critical to living a truly satisfying life. Sleeping when you're tired can clear the stress and anxiety that keep you from realizing the peace that's deep inside you.

The American business culture has typically shunned the need for sleep, as if it's a sign of weakness.

Wearing our busyness like a badge of honor, as if it's a sign of virility, many of us herald entrepreneurs and business titans for sleeping only 3–5 hours a night. We believe that no matter how tired we are, we have to forgo sleep to compete in the global marketplace that makes it possible to shop, bank, talk, and work 24 hours a day, seven days a week.[40]

You can go without sleep for a while, and not notice the effects, but they will catch up with you.

Arianna Huffington, the founder of The Huffington Post, learned that the hard way. When the online news aggregator was still in its early days, Arianna felt that it needed her constant attention. She also had two daughters to care for. This left Arianna little time to sleep, sometimes functioning on only two or three hours sleep a night. She felt she was managing it all, until one day she collapsed from exhaustion and broke her cheekbone in the fall. This woke her up to changes she needed to make in her life. She's now a great champion of sleep.[41]

There are some folks who have a gene mutation known as hDEC2 that enables them to function well on little sleep, but they aren't the norm. Perhaps some of the entrepreneurs and CEOs we point to as beacons of perpetual wakefulness have this gene. You probably don't. If you need caffeine carbs, or sugar to get you through your day, if you feel sluggish or irritable more often than you'd like, you can be pretty sure you don't have it. What you do have is a need for more sleep.

I was one of the crazies who thought sleep was for sissies. I now know that the opposite is true.

For most of my life, I was a champion at not sleeping. I never wanted to miss a thing. Outlasting all babysitters in the "who can stay up later" competition, I never developed good sleep habits. The pattern continued into my adult years.

My life wasn't just full. It was bursting at the seams with a robust career, volunteer commitments, an active social life and lots of exercise. Running businesses isn't always a picnic and being over committed creates its own pressure. I had a ton of fun, but I also had bucket loads of stress.

What was consistently lacking in my life was sleep. I'd jump out of bed each morning, after too few hours, with my mind racing ahead before my feet hit the floor.

After a few decades of living this way, there was too much stress with too little recovery. In my mid 30s an autoimmune disease knocked me off my feet and right into bed.

I was finishing my Master's degree, opening a new business, renovating my house, and going through a breakup. I didn't give myself recovery time. I just kept pushing harder. Throughout it all, I slept very little.

Lack of sleep didn't give me the disease. It had been in my cells. But we can all affect our DNA through lifestyle choices. We can turn some genes on and others off, with our behavior. Without giving my body a chance to repair and heal itself from stress each day, I was giving my genes a little nudge in the direction of illness.

I went from full on to full stop. I had to leave work, and bow out of volunteering. I rarely saw my friends. For several years I could barely get out of bed. I was ashamed of how much sleep I needed.

As I've recovered I've discovered that sleep makes you strong. It's the secret fuel for your super hero powers.

Even the strongest and fastest animals on the planet spend more than half their life asleep. Maybe that's the secret to their speed and strength. It certainly fuels it.

These days I love to give my thoughts and body to the deep relaxation of sleep. I've developed habits for morning and night that honor sleep as a sacred ritual in my life. I take naps. Illness forced me to have the tough conversations with myself about what matters most.

I am no longer too busy, nor too lazy, to sleep.

Just because everyone else is sleep deprived, that doesn't make it right.

Most of the clients I've worked with have at some point expressed overwork, exhaustion, and lack of drive to do the things they really want. Some of my tired clients push themselves to stay busy so they won't feel how exhausted they are. They jack themselves up on caffeine, sugar, adrenaline, and willpower, the way I used to.

Some are afraid that if they stop to rest they may never get started again. They've bought into the belief that giving into their need for sleep, and indulging in the pleasure of rest, will somehow get in the way of serving their families, their business and the world.

Clients come to me because they want some part of their life to be better. Whether they want to build an empire, reduce their anxiety, have more love in their life, or less fat on their ass I always ask, "How's your sleep?" Quite frequently they answer, "It sucks."

When you're not getting enough sleep, the rest of your life will be a struggle. If my client isn't sleeping well, I always make that a priority.

Philosopher Jiddu Krishnamurti said, "It is no measure of health to be well adjusted to a profoundly sick society." I invite my clients to go against the tide of our sick society and embrace sleep as a normal and pleasurable part of life. Sleep is a solid foundation upon which to build everything else you want.

Though the fear of missing out can be overwhelming at first, my clients find that their energy and productivity are greatly enhanced by more sleep. Relationships are more enjoyable and business ideas flourish. Addictions ease and anxiety drops. All of life is easier.

If I offered you a pill that promised this, I could charge a fortune and you'd probably do everything in your power to get it. Sleep has all these benefits and no ugly side effects. Oh, and did I mention? It's free.

You'll do more of what you want to do when you're sleeping well.

Like a tree that goes dormant through the winter to return each spring with luscious fruits, you're able to live your juiciest life and give your ripest gifts, when you're rested.

Honor your natural rhythm and you'll feel more energized.

You're designed to live in sync with the rhythms of nature. Tiredness and wakefulness are determined by your circadian rhythm, which is controlled by a part of your brain that responds to light.[42]

That's why you feel most alert when the sun is shining, and you get sleepy when it's dark.

If you were living as your ancient ancestors did, you'd wake with the rising sun in the morning and sit by the dim light of fire at night, before going to sleep in darkness. This pattern keeps your circadian rhythm in balance.

I experienced this when I lived in Mexico. If I was out when the sun set I walked home under the darkening sky, and climbed the hill to my house by the light of the moon. The changing light hushed the town and calmed my body. At home I'd do yoga and meditate by candlelight before going to bed. The routine quieted my mind and prepared me for sleep.

You can support your rhythm by sleeping in a dark room and easing into daylight when you wake up. If you're like most North Americans, you're more likely to veg out in front of the tv or computer before going to bed.

While it can feel good to finally flop on the couch and be done with the day, the blue tint light from the screen stimulates your brain and suppresses melatonin, the hormone that helps you sleep. It overrides your natural rhythm that would tell you it's time for bed.

Suppressing melatonin with the light not only delays your sleep, it can affect your Rapid Eye Movement, (dream state), throughout the night. That leaves you more tired and stressed, less positive and productive. You're more likely to need stimulants in the day, and crash in front of a screen again at night. The cycle continues, creating more stress and fatigue.[37]

In general, teens need more sleep than adults. Recent research shows that young people who text an hour before going to bed are less likely to have a good night's sleep, and poor sleep can lead to depression, increased car accidents, and a decrease in physical and mental health and memory.[43]

Unplugging technology an hour or more before going to bed can help them wind down, and get the sleep they need. Teaching them by example would do wonders for you too. Try unplugging as a family as early as possible before your kids' bedtime, and see if getting to sleep becomes easier for everyone. Dim the lights, use candles instead, play games, go for a walk and see the eerie blue light shining in your neighbors' homes.

If you or your kids have to be in front of a screen in the evening consider using blue tint blocking glasses. (Go to www.debrajoy.me/resources for the Resource Guide)

Though they'll block the blue light that suppresses your melatonin it won't stop you from being stimulated by the interaction. Whenever possible, unplugging is the better choice.

The remedy for being stressed out, overweight, fatigued and irritable may be as simple as getting more sleep.

Simple sure. But easy? Hmmmm....

You've got to be willing to go against the norm, as all great adventurers and leaders have done. You're going to be constantly bombarded by messages to stay up late, wake up early, work hard, play hard, push through your limits, and go for it.. all the time.

Some of the smartest and most successful among us honor their sleep.

Facebook's COO, Sheryl Strandberg, is currently one of the highest paid executives in Silicon Valley, and she's in bed every night by 9:30pm. First Lady Michelle Obama goes to bed early so she can get up and workout before her busy day starts. Benjamin Franklin, Maya Angelou, and Kurt Vonnegut were all in bed by 10:00pm... but not together.

If you've been overriding your body's messages that you need to rest, you'll probably need to create some hard-core sleep habits, until you find your rhythm again.

Turn sleep into a sacred ritual.

Rituals elevate an event from the ordinary to the extraordinary. They help you drop out of your fast-forward life for a moment. They focus your attention, soften your gaze and make you present.

Without the ritual, a Japanese tea ceremony is just hot liquid being poured into a cup. It's the ritual that raises consciousness.

Sleep can become a sacred practice, out of ordinary time and space. Like meditation, it may not be exquisite every night, but over years, with practice, it can change your brain in ways that enhance your life.

Dr. Pelayo, professor of sleep medicine at Stanford School of Medicine, says "The best sleepers in our society are 8-year-olds, who still have rules about bedtimes and go to bed without any worries."

Bedtime routines help kids' brains and bodies shift from activity to inactivity. It'll do the same for you.

Having a bath, putting on pajamas, tucking into bed and reading a story, are all rituals that calm a child's thinking, and prepare her for sleep.

While I can't promise you the worry-free life of an eight-year-old, a simple bedtime routine, repeated nightly 10 – 30 minutes before you want to be asleep, will help you shift from doing to non-doing.

Just make sure your routine is calming, rather than stimulating. Do the same thing every night and it will start lulling you to sleep.

The number one reason for insomnia is anxiety.[24] The simplest way to over come anxiety is breathing. You can use some of the practices in Breathe as part of your bedtime ritual. A little bit of breathing can do wonders for your sleep. I've also included a guided meditation in the following link: www.debrajoy.me/practices. You can use it to relax yourself back to sleep.

Waking in the middle of the night is a cause of anxiety for some, but it's actually quite natural. Before the early 1800's it was common to have two sleeps a night, broken by a gap of a few hours. During this time people would read by candlelight, pray, make love, or talk.

Our early ancestors would have been prey when they were sleeping outdoors. It makes sense that we'd naturally wake at different times, as a matter of survival for the tribe.

If you wake often in the middle of the night, and aren't getting enough sleep, try going to bed earlier and allow yourself two sleeps, as a way to honor what your body wants to do.

Then when you wake, do something relaxing. Keep the lights low. Journal, meditate, plan out your day. Avoid checking the time and worrying about your sleep.

If late nights are dimming your bright light, it may seem like sleeping in when you can is the cure, but you'll actually do better sticking with the same wake time and adjusting your evening schedule to get the sleep you need.

A great day starts the night before.

Decide on the time you'd like to wake. Move your bedtime up in half hour increments, a week at a time, until you're getting enough sleep to really thrive; able to wake at your regular time without an alarm, feeling refreshed. Once you've found a bedtime that gives you the sleep you need, stick to it until it becomes a habit.

Biomechanist and author, Katy Bowman says, "Going to bed early is like sleeping in at the other end". When you develop good sleep habits you can start to feel when your body wants to go to sleep and adjust it as your body needs. If you're zoning out with television or internet, and overriding your body's signals, you can't yet trust yourself to feel when your body is tired.

It's easy to lose track of time at night when you're living by artificial light. Before you know it it's way past your bedtime. I recommend my clients set an alarm on their phone that rings every night at the same time, reminding them it's time to go to sleep, as a way of supporting a new healthy habit.

At the end of a long day you may lack the willpower to turn off the tv, shut down your computer, or put away your phone, even with a reminder. For clients who struggle with technology late into the night, I recommend an electronic timer. (Go to www.debrajoy.me/resources.) They set it to turn off their television and internet at the same time every night - the time they'd like to go to bed. If they choose to stay up later one night, they can get up, go to the outlet, and override the timer, turning everything back on. That automatic shut down is all most people need to start getting sleep at the time they know is best.

It can be helpful to track what it is you're staying up late to do. Is it really adding to the overall quality of your life? What's one thing you could give up to have more sleep and enjoy life more? Could you move an activity to another time during the day, and get to bed earlier?

Keeping a regular schedule to sleep and wake will do wonders for your energy, libido, creativity, productivity, and moods. It will reduce your tension and anxiety.

Varying the times you wake up and go to bed is like giving yourself jet lag.

Even one night of insufficient sleep is enough to upset your sleep rhythm, but life will get in the way of your best intentions.

Special events, holidays, and work will take precedence over a good night's sleep at times. And they should. Life should be full of spontaneity and joy. When these special events keep you up late, return to your regular schedule to get your body back on track, as soon as you can.

If possible, stick with your regular wake time, even the nights you go to bed too late. Go to bed earlier the next night, and for a few nights if needed, to make up that sleep debt. That will help you slip back into the right track more easily.

Turn your bedroom into a sanctuary to enhance your sleep.

You don't have to sleep in a temple, but the simple act of clearing counters, removing clutter, or having a soothing image to look at, can support your sleep.

Deanna was supposed to be implementing a strategy to take her business to the next level, but something was stopping her from moving forward. She was showing up tired to all of our sessions.

When I asked her about her sleep, she said it was fitful.

She had trouble falling asleep, she'd often wake during the night, and was awake far earlier than she wanted to be. She wanted to avoid talking about sleep and focus on her business, but I can be a real pain in the ass sometimes, and I wouldn't let it go.

I told Diane to relax on her bed and describe what she saw.

Furniture she'd inherited filled most of the space. The floor was littered with clothes, books, and kids' toys. A basket overflowed with clean laundry, waiting to be put away. Spreadsheets and fabric samples were on the other side of the king bed.

I asked her to describe how it all made her feel.

The stuff on the floor and laundry in the basket were demanding her attention. She'd kept the furniture out of obligation, but had never liked it. It was heavy and dark, and made the room feel cramped. The fabric samples got her excited and made her want to dive into work. None of this felt conducive to sleep.

I asked her to imagine what a sanctuary would feel like.

With her eyes closed, she was able to describe it. I recommended that Deanna schedule a chunk of time, even stealing some away from work, to turn her bedroom into that sanctuary as best she could.

Lying on her bed, surrounded by stuff, she reluctantly agreed. She pulled everything out of her room except the bed. She decided to paint the walls a soothing color. She then considered each item before bringing it back in. If it wasn't needed, and didn't contribute to rest and relaxation, she found a place for it somewhere else in the house, or put it in a pile in the garage to give away. She made room in the closet for the laundry basket so she could close the door and have it out of site. Even the flat screen that had been a fixture on their dresser for years was now banished from the bedroom.

With the room free of clutter and distraction, Deanna found it easier to rest.

Her sleep improved over time. She developed simple evening and morning routines that felt easier in a space free of clutter. Without the television or computers in the room, she and Dave connected more as a couple in their private space.

With her sleep improving, and her energy returning, it was easier to focus on the next stages of her business, and come up with creative, strategic ideas.

Allow yourself this little luxury. Turn your bedroom into a sanctuary for sleep and sex. You don't have to do it all at once. Start with one simple change that would make a difference.

Clear clutter. Your room should be peaceful.

Make it a no phone zone. If you use your phone for the alarm, put it on airplane mode so you won't be disturbed. If there's someone who may need to reach you in case of an emergency, set the Do Not Disturb feature and allow only their call to come through when Do Not Disturb is engaged. My phone goes into Do Not Disturb every night automatically from 9:00pm – 7:00am.

Make it dark. Even a bit of light can disrupt your circadian rhythms. Black out curtains can help. (Go to www.debrajoy.me/resources.)

Keep it cool. Set your thermostat to 68 degrees or less. You'll sleep better when your core temperature is cool.

Then lay back, relax, and surrender to what may possibly be "the best meditation" every night.

If you want to feel like a super hero, nap to fuel your super powers.

The mighty Grizzly Bear sleeps an average of 5 months a year, and naps during the summer days. The cheetah is the fastest animal on land, able to run 70 miles an hour. She sleeps 13 hours a night and then naps during the day. We are the only animals on the planet that try to get all of our sleep at once.[44]

In the 90s, NASA recognized sleep's crucial role in performance and introduced short naps as part of the astronauts' workdays. Performance skyrocketed. A mere 20 minute nap restored energy, improved focus and boosted moods. No wonder it's called the Power Nap.

Though it was a completely foreign ritual for American professionals at the time of NASA's introduction of naps, many cultures have thrived with long afternoon naps for centuries.

For a few hours after lunch each day business ceases, stores close, and families gather for a meal and some rest. These long breaks are called siestas. Workers return later in the day refreshed and alert.

The first time I encountered a siesta I was a young girl traveling in Mexico with my friend's family. I was stunned when the restaurant closed just as we were finishing our lunch. Stores locked up and the streets were empty. The town was hushed, except for the soft strumming of a guitar floating towards us from a dusty alley. There was nothing left for us to do but rest. I had never experienced anything like it. The slow, silent memory lives in my body to this day.

Like making your own bone broth or brewing beer in small batches, the ancient practice of napping is becoming hip again.

After her exhausted collapse, Arianna Huffington installed nap spaces at Huffington Post offices. Though employees were reluctant at first, the spaces are now often filled with power nappers.

Nike, Google, The New York Times, and many other American companies have also created nap positive cultures. Napping has become an accepted policy at many Japanese companies as well. Though nap rooms or pods are a far cry from a siesta, it's a big step in the right direction.

Naps can do more than just boost your energy. They can truly set you free.

I'm a recovering sugar addict and I used to crave sweet stuff every afternoon. As if I'd been overtaken by a demon, I'd inhale cookies into my gaping maw, unable to stop myself.

Eventually I stopped to breathe and feel what was really going on when these zombie-like trances took me over. As I became aware of what was happening, I realized that I was just tired. Deeply tired. Totally freaking exhausted. And rather than go to sleep I wanted to keep doing whatever I was doing. Afraid, once again, of missing out.

Once I became aware of what was going on, I could choose differently. And I did.

I started scheduling an afternoon nap. Voila - my sugar cravings vanished. At this point in my life I no longer schedule an afternoon nap. I will enjoy one if I need it. I can sense when my energy is slipping and now just lying on the ground for 10 minutes, completely letting go, can be enough to revive me at times.

Listening to my body's true craving for rest, and giving myself what I really needed, enabled me to live in sync with my rhythm, rather than fight against it. The constant afternoon sugar cravings have vanished.

If you've tried napping before only to wake feeling groggy, you're not alone. Maybe you don't know about the magic numbers of naps: 20 and 90.

A 20 minute nap will be a quick reset to restore your energy. A nap of 90 minutes or more, like a siesta, will allow your brain to get into

REM state.

The grey zone between 20 and 90 minutes is zombie land. If you wake during that time you're likely to feel like the walking dead. If you can't sleep for 90 minutes or longer, set an alarm for 20 minutes. This way you'll wake refreshed. Even a six minute nap can improve your memory and problem solving.[45]

Some people worry that if they nap they'll have trouble sleeping. Napping in the day can actually improve your sleep at night, as long as it's at least three hours before your bedtime.[24]

Just some quiet time can give you the rest you need.

Some clients balk when I recommend they adopt a regular bedtime or take naps in the day. They feel belittled by the suggestion, even when they're complaining weekly about being tired, grumpy, and not at their best.

Suzanne was no different. Her athletic clothing business was starting to take off. With her staff fulfilling orders, she was still able to do most of her work from home. She'd never had her own business before, and though she had an assistant and other staff working with her, the final decision was always hers to make.

She often felt overwhelmed enough to paralyze her at times. I suggested that movement would help shake her out of overwhelm, but she was too fatigued to even try.

As we reviewed how she spent her days, I saw that she was glued to technology, and always available to her company. She'd wake after a restless night and jump on the computer to check orders that had come in. After getting her eight year old daughter fed and off to school, she'd sit back in front of the computer for several hours without a break. To make it through her mid afternoon energy dip she'd grab a coffee and cookies, collapse on the couch and cruise her company's social media sites, adding comments and responding to followers. She was too tired to do anything else.

After making dinner and spending time with her daughter, she'd jump back online and deal with more business or watch a movie until she went to bed.

When I recommended Suzanne try a nap instead of her coffee and sugar break in the afternoon, she scoffed at the idea.

But as the weeks went by and she found herself getting more irritated by little things, and even snapping at her daughter, she was willing to try something different.

She agreed to give herself quiet time.

When her daughter was young, Suzanne set up quiet time for her. She could do whatever she wanted in her bedroom; read or play with toys, but she had to stay in her room for half an hour, and she had to be quiet. Suzanne would close the curtains, dim the light and shut the door. Nine times out of ten her daughter fell asleep.

As an experiment, Suzanne gave herself the same guidelines. At 1:00pm each day she'd power down her technology, go into her room with a cup of herbal tea, pull down the blinds and rest. She gave herself permission to write or read if she wanted, but every afternoon she fell asleep. Some days she was shocked to discover she'd slept for a few hours. The first few times she woke in a panic. She was surprised, and even a little disappointed, to learn that everything was running fine. There was no problem too big that couldn't wait for her return.

Suzanne turned this into a ritual.

She'd set her alarm for half an hour, sometimes she'd sleep, and other times she'd just relax. After quiet time, Suzanne felt more energized for her business and her daughter. Creative ideas started flowing again.

After several months of the quiet time ritual, I recommended Suzanne begin to move. Now she felt ready. She started taking short breaks every 90 minutes, dancing, stretching, or shaking her body. This helped her move through periods of overwhelm and infused some fun into her workdays.

Once those practices were comfortably in place, she began walking for half an hour a day. The added movement helped boost her energy and her mood. She was surprised that resting and moving more, which both took her away from her work, actually made her more focused and productive in her work time.

She was getting more done in less time, and feeling better about herself. And it all began by getting the rest she needed.

If getting away from work to take a nap is not an option take five slow breaths, exhale completely and feel the breath come back in your body.[27] You'll give your nervous system some rest. (You can use the guided meditation at: www.debrajoy.me/practices).

When you're properly nourished with sleep you thrive.

Your mind is relaxed and sharp, your thinking is creative and positive. You're more compassionate with yourself and kinder towards others. You feel more alive and happy. Your relationships flourish.

With proper rest it's easier to hear your heart's desire and be guided by your inner wisdom.

I offer the following practices to develop sleep habits that will enable you to connect with your rhythm once again. Explore the practices and discover which work best for you.

Even once some become habits, it's important to pay attention to what your body really wants in the moment, and surrender to that. Your circadian rhythms will change over time and living in sync requires you to pay attention to how you feel, rather than follow a rigid routine.

SLEEP

PRACTICES

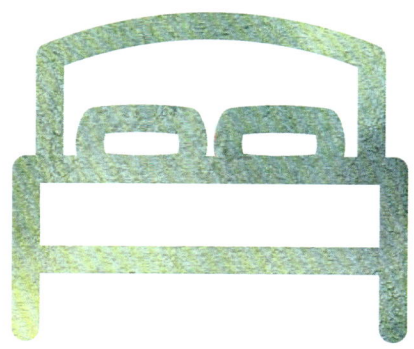

– HAVE REGULAR TIMES TO SLEEP AND WAKE –

Having a regular time to sleep and wake is one of the best things you can do to support your circadian rhythm, optimize your energy, productivity, relationships and moods. If you decide to stay up past your optimal bedtime, just make it a conscious choice and feel good about your choice.

 Start by knowing when you want to wake up. Then work backwards.

 Adjust your bedtime in half hour increments, for a week or more at a time, until you find the bedtime that enables you to wake at your desired time, with an alarm, feeling rested.

 Unplug from technology at least an hour before your bedtime to enhance your sleep.

 Stick with this sleep and wake schedule every day, as best you can. Plan your evenings in advance so you can get to sleep at the right time.

There will be special events that keep you up past your desired time. Enjoy them. Take a nap the next day if you can. Go to bed earlier for a few nights to make up the lost sleep. Stick with your regular wake time.

– SET YOUR SLEEP ALARMS –

Ask yourself "What's the best time for me to go to sleep?"

Answer it honestly.

When I ask my clients this question, some know the right answer immediately, even if they are going to bed much later than that.

Then ask, "What will be different if I go to sleep at this time?"

That's your WHY. You want to know why you'd go to sleep at that time. Unless you can imagine the difference it will make, it may be hard to make the changes you want. Knowing can help you stay motivated.

Once you know the right time for you, and why, work backwards from there. Set your alarms.

 Set an alarm on your phone or watch for 30 minutes before you want to go to bed.

 When this rings it's a reminder to stop what you're doing and get ready for sleep.

 Do your bedtime routine.

 Go to sleep.

Sounds simple, but it can be a real challenge to make yourself go to bed. You may experience all sorts of childish rebellion rise up inside you. "I don't have to." "You're not the boss of me." "I'll do what I want."

You're determining what's best for you. Nobody else. So when you're rebelling against going to sleep, know that you're fighting what you want for yourself.

That's why it's important to know why you're doing it.

If you try this and still can't make yourself go to bed, try this step to prepare you.

Turn your WHY into a mantra. If you said, "I'll have more energy and feel happier tomorrow" that's your mantra.

 Set your alarm for the time you want to go to bed.

 When it rings, say your mantra, "I'll have more energy and feel happier tomorrow if I go to bed right now."

 Notice how you feel.

 Go to bed, or keep doing what you're doing.

Just saying the mantra and noticing how you feel is enough. You can do this for a week or more as a precursor to actually going to sleep at the time you'd like.

When I've offered this practice to clients it's helped them realize they aren't fighting anyone else by staying up late. They can tap into their own desire for sleep.

– Turn off Technology –

If you're using the alarm system to go to sleep it can help to have an alarm to remind you to power down technology as well.

 Know what time you want to go to bed.

 Set an alarm to power down your technology one, two or more hours before that time.

 Do something relaxing and enjoyable instead of being in front of a screen.

- Spend time with loved ones, read, relax.
- It's best if you can start to wind down and dim lights as it gets closer to sleep time.

 Go to bed at your desired time, after your nighttime routine.

If you try this idea but find yourself hooked to technology long after your alarm has rung, it may help to have your outlet on a timer, so that it automatically turns off. (Go to www.debrajoy.me/resources for the Resource Guide)

Options:
If you decide to override the technology shut down sometimes, wear blue light blocking glasses to support your circadian rhythm and a good night sleep. (Go to www.debrajoy.me/resources for the Resource Guide)

You can also install f.lux on your computer for free. It will change the color of your computer screen to match the time of day—warm at night and cool and bright in the day. (Go to www.debrajoy.me/resources for the Resource Guide)

While you may avoid the blue light affects, just being engaged with technology can stimulate your brain in a way that impacts deep sleep. Turning off technology is the best choice.

– Practice a Bedtime Ritual –

Performing a simple ritual is a way to turn something ordinary into something sacred with your presence. Right before you go to sleep is a perfect time for this, as it quiets your mind.

Keep the ritual as simple and short as possible so that it's easy to do, even if you're sleeping away from home.

Choose a ritual that feels positive, and won't tax your brain. Do it regularly.

Some ideas are:

- Meditate for 2 - 10 minutes to clear your mind.
- Pray.
- Write out things you accomplished in the day, even the simplest task. Reflect on how good it feels to get those things done.
- Write about one thing you're grateful for today and how it made you feel.
- Write your top three priorities for tomorrow, so you clear those things from your mind and wake up with focus.
- Have a bath with epsom salts. The magnesium will help you sleep.
- Apply a body lotion and pay attention to how it feels and smells. One with magnesium can support your sleep (Go to www.debrajoy.me/resources for the Resource Guide)
- Read from a book that makes you feel good.

Choose just one. Habits are formed best one at a time, performed at the same time each day. Commit to the ritual every single night. If you miss a night, begin it again the very next night.

– Have a Nap or Quiet Time –

A nap of 20 minutes or less, might be the key to a better life. Remember that Dr. Edlund says even a 6 minute nap will refresh you.

You might not be able to nap every day, but giving yourself 20 minutes of quiet time, or lying in savasana for even 6 minutes, can do wonders for your creativity, productivity, and peace of mind.

 Schedule a break into your day. If it's planned, you're more likely to do it.

 Set an alarm for 20 minutes so that you don't wake up in the zombie zone.

 If you can't fall asleep, lie in savasana for 6 minutes or more. It's a yoga pose, also called corpse pose.

- Lie on your back with your arms at your side.

- Close your eyes and let your body completely relax.

- Pay attention to your breathing. With each exhale let your body drop down into the ground.

 Try scheduling this rest time into your day for a week and see how it works for you. Choose the time in the day when your energy usually drops.

– Turn your Bedroom into a Sanctuary –

When you turn your bedroom into a sanctuary, you honor your sleep, (and possibly sex), as something sacred. You revere the mysterious process that heals, nourishes, and informs your body, brain, and soul.

You want your sanctuary to be restful, cool and dark, when you go to sleep.

 Close your eyes and imagine how a sleep sanctuary would look and feel. Don't think of your bedroom as it is. Let your mind run wild. Get as specific as you can in your imagination. Notice how this sanctuary makes you feel.

 Make the simplest changes that most support the feeling of being in a sanctuary.

- Remove everything that doesn't support the look and feel of a sleep sanctuary. Find homes for these objects somewhere else in your house, or give them away.

- Then carefully add colors, objects, and blank spaces that make your room feel more like the sanctuary of your meditation. This could be deep browns, books of poetry, blood reds, and crystals. It might be all white.

- Just start with one change if you don't have much time to make changes.

 Make a weekly practice of cleaning your sanctuary. Wash your sheets. Remove any items that have found their way into your temple of sleep and sex that don't belong there.

You can treat this as a spiritual practice, and give your full attention to it, noticing the changes in the feel of the room as you clear its energy.

You determine what is sacred and peaceful for you. You decide how your sanctuary should look and feel. Purchase the most comfortable sheets, pillows, and duvets you can. Invest in sumptuous pajamas. Upgrade your bed if that's needed. Get drapes or blinds that enable you to darken the room completely. Add plants or flowers as you please. It's your sanctuary.

(Go to www.debrajoy.me/resources for ways to darken your space)

– YOUR PRACTICE –

WHAT:

_____

Name this practice

WHY:

_____

_____

What do you expect to gain from this practice?
Knowing why you're doing it will help keep you motivated.

BREAK YOUR PRACTICE DOWN INTO VERY SIMPLE STEPS.

1. _____

   _____

2. _____

   _____

3. _____

   _____

4. _____

   _____

TRIGGER:

_____

When developing a new habit it's best to do it every day, at the same time if possible, and it's
important to have something that reminds you, or triggers you to do it.

What will trigger you to do this practice?

- NOTES -

MOVE

"If you just set people in motion
they'll heal themselves."

– Gabrielle Roth

Something magical happens when you see a hummingbird flapping its wings, watch waves crashing on a shore, track a baby taking his first steps, or gaze at the sun dipping slowly into the horizon.

The movement around you can touch something inside you. You might feel the rise, the struggle, the stutter, the flutter, or the slow, peaceful decent resonating in you. You may even say it moves you.

There's a magnificence and beauty to natural movement that inspires.

You're already moving.

Right now your lungs are expanding and contracting. Your heart is pumping oxygen through your body. Old cells are dying, while new cells are being born. Your intestines are absorbing nutrients and pushing out what you don't need. You've been moving since you were in your mother's womb.

Your body knows what to do and how to do it.

It wants to move in all kinds of ways: crouch, stretch, crawl, walk, sprint, punch, dance, and embrace. At times it wants to explode with energy, and other times it wants to unfurl slowly and sensuously.

Your body has an innate wisdom that will naturally move you in ways that are nourishing, efficient, and pleasurable, if you will let it.

Movement makes you feel good.

You know how great you feel when you come home from a long walk or run. After stressing your body against gravity and the elements, you feel that "good tired" at the end of the day.

Movement doesn't have to be big and showy to feel good.

Right now as you're reading this, move your body in any way that feels good to you. You might roll your shoulders, move your head from side to side, arch your back and stretch, breathe deeply, or take your eyes off the page and look around.

Notice how you feel after just this little bit of movement. You may be energized, more relaxed, and comfortable. Or you may feel tired in a way you hadn't noticed before.

Authentic movement will connect you to yourself. To move authentically is to follow your body's impulses. To do that you must become aware.

That moment of awareness is a portal to your true self.

Movement is a proven treatment for depression.

Exercise releases endorphins that boost your mood long after the movement is over. It also improves your focus.[26]

Dr. John Ratey, expert in neuropsychiatry and author of Spark - The Revolutionary New Science of Exercise and the Brain, says that exercise, "is like taking a little bit of Prozac and a little bit of Ritalin." Prozac is an anti-depressant and Ritalin is a drug to treat ADHD.[26] If you take drugs that are improving your life, I'm not suggesting you ditch them.

If you want to be happier and more focused, try moving more. Dr. Ratey calls exercise Miracle-Gro for the brain.

Movement makes you smarter.

In Spark, Ratey shares the story of a school in Naperville, Ill. They began an optional Zero Hour PE class to see if exercising before school would give kids a boost in their reading ability and other subjects.

At the end of the semester, Zero Hour participants showed a 17% improvement in reading and comprehension, compared with a 10.7% improvement for students who opted to sleep in and take regular PE.

The results were so intriguing that the administration incorporated Zero Hour into the high school curriculum as a first-period literacy class called Learning Readiness PE.[26] The guidance counselors suggested that all students schedule their hardest subjects immediately after PE to capitalize on the benefits of exercise.

Phil Lawler was the PE teacher who brought about this change in the Naperville high school. His inspiration came from a newspaper article in 1990 that said the health of US children was declining due to inactivity. Sadly since that report came out, most children and adults have become even less active.

Movement is more than just exercise.

To counteract our sedentary lives, many people exercise. If you exercise regularly, keep it up. The benefits are vital to living a good life. In the past I've been a personal trainer, aerobics instructor, and yoga teacher, so I'm not down on exercise. But exercise offers only a limited aspect of the authentic movement alive in your DNA.

You were born with the capacity for a vast range of motion.

Until recently your survival would have depended on a life full of movement. Satisfying your body's need for water, food, shelter, and sex required daily walking, running, and crouching to forage, hunt, carry, and create.

For thousands of years your ancestors operated this way, spending most of their lives in motion. This created healthy, robust, and flexible bodies.[27]

If exercise is your main source of movement you're limiting what you're capable of. Since your body and mind are interconnected, the fluidity and flexibility of one affects the other. Spontaneous, natural, pleasure driven movements fuel your brain for growth and creativity. Repetitive, linear movements can keep you stuck in repetitive, linear thinking.

Movement is more than just physical.

Natural movement is a way of being. It's a physical expression of your spirit. Movement is all the cosmos and mystery of the universe funneling energy through your body.

All you have to do is allow it.

It's a way to connect with the divine universal life force that lives within you, and be guided by it. Though it sounds like a paradox, when you pay attention to internal sensations, and follow the movement, it can guide you to the eternal stillness within you. That place of pure peace.

Many spiritual practices use movement to worship, become present, and connect with the divine.

There are walking meditations. Sufis whirl. And in the Christian church where I spent several years, I danced wildly in the aisles, shedding ideas and thoughts, until there was nothing left of me but the ecstatic expanse of emptiness.

There isn't one way to move that's more spiritual than another.

Just because yoga works for some, doesn't mean it's the path for you. Kick-boxing, gardening, or taking a deep breath, can all be portals to your divine self, if you just pay attention.

Wake up your body and awaken yourself.

When you let the pleasure of movement be your guide, you access your primal nature, intuition and creativity.

Years ago I was working with my colleagues on a presentation for a large corporation. We had a week to complete the project and deliver our results to the board. One of the members of our team was wise enough to make us start by sharing our unique skills and how we worked best.

In that first meeting I told the others that I needed to move, and would like to take breaks to do that.

When I left the group every afternoon to move my body, they'd all be huddled together in the office, mind mapping, problem solving, and tapping at their key boards. The times they were laughing and having fun I felt like I was missing out by taking this time for myself. The times they were tense with anxiety, worried about our deadline, I felt guilty for leaving them.

At the time I was a workaholic who was more likely to plow through without stopping, believing it was the more efficient way to perform, but I was learning new habits to overcome my obsessive ways.

No matter how my thoughts tried to guilt me into working through, I changed my clothes and headed for the gym in the woods behind our office every day. While running, stretching, walking, dancing, and lifting weights, I would focus on my body and breath moving in sync.

Often during these breaks ideas would come to me for our project, seemingly out of nowhere; an answer to a problem or a new way of doing things. I could tap into some source I wasn't able to access sitting at the boardroom table.

I always returned with renewed energy and enthusiasm while the others were fading in their place.

I was far more creative, productive, and focused after every time I took a break to move. The exercise I did then was far more structured and less natural than what I would do today, but the break for movement, and time in nature, was a step in the right direction.

I encourage my clients to move several times throughout the day, doing whatever feels good at the time. Not just as a form of exercise, but as a way of connecting with themselves. To get clear, feel lighter, and hear their own guidance.

Authentic movement helps you get unstuck.

Maria was suffocating under the weight of the terrible twins— procrastination and overwhelm. As a single mom and business owner, she always had lots to do for her business and in her home. On a coaching call she said she felt like a hamster running on a wheel.

I asked her to get up do exactly that - run like a hamster on a wheel. She even held her arms out in front of her, pulling each rung down as she ran. She ran faster and faster. Imagining herself on the wheel. I asked her to jump off the wheel and notice where she'd run if she wasn't caged. She imagined running to an open field, through a meadow. Under a big cloudless sky she could breathe. She stopped and sat down in the tall grass. The moment she stopped she felt more energized.

When we got back to work she knew what to focus on first. She was able to take me through her list of things she would do, and explain why she'd do each one.

I often use movement to get out of my head and connect with my true self. When I do that it's easier to feel my own joy and express my true self.

I recommend short bursts of movement for clients throughout their day. It improves energy and also helps release stress that can build up. (See Release for more on this.)

Years ago I co-hosted an awards ceremony. I've never enjoyed public speaking, so I stood back-stage trying to calm my nerves, while 1,000 people found their seats, and the band played upbeat music. My heart was pounding, my jaw was clenched, and my hands were balled into tight fists. I didn't want to walk out on stage.

I thought I might throw up.

I closed my eyes and dropped my head, while producers with headsets walked around me. As I turned my focus from the outer world to my inner world, I felt my body's desire to move.

I stood behind the curtain, hidden from the audience, and danced. With closed eyes I followed by body's impulses.

In the distance I heard two voices. "What's she doing?" "Looks like she's dancing." But I didn't care. I was swept up by the beat and the energy of my body moving freely.

The band kept playing as someone announced my name, so I danced my way onto the stage. I sensed if I stopped I might be paralyzed by fear. Dancing wasn't what we'd planned, but it felt completely natural, and as long as I was moving I was free.

Later in the show I introduced a bank CEO who unexpectedly danced with me when he got on stage. By starting with what was true for me it seemed I set others free as well. I got lots of feedback from presenters and audience members that the night was a ton of fun.

The dancing surprised everyone and added a flavor of delight.

I was just doing what was right for me. The movement got me unstuck. It enabled me to connect with myself, to become present and to connect with my co-presenters and audience members as well.

Someone else may have moved a different way that was true for her, and she would have brought her true self to the show. If you're about to do something challenging, if you're stressed, or feeling stuck in your life, I suggest you move more.

Sedentary living shapes your body.

It's only been a fraction of time in our human evolution that innovations have allowed us a more sedentary life.

We've gone from spending days hunting, gathering and preparing our food, to clicking a button on a phone that delivers prepared meals to our doors. This has freed up time and energy to forge scientific advancements along with great works of art, but it's disconnected us from our bodies in profound ways.

The comforts of modern life have forced your body into a dulled state.

Shoes limit the natural movement of your feet. Your car, office chair, and living room couch keep you in the same seated position most of the day. Your mattress fits to the contours of your body, holding you in place all night.

Your natural movements have become restricted.

What shapes your body shapes your thoughts and moods.

Have you ever looked into the empty eyes of a tiger sitting on a cement floor behind metal bars, or watched caged monkeys rocking back and forth for hours at a time? Even in "good zoos," elephants, giraffes, big cats and primates exhibit abnormal behavior because they aren't able to live naturally.

Like caged animals, we limit our natural movements by driving instead of walking, texting instead of visiting and watching instead of participating. None of this is natural.

Our bodies are responding with heart disease, diabetes, osteoporosis, obesity, hypertension, depression, and even certain cancers.

In her book, Move Your DNA, bio-mechanist Katy Bowman gives an example of captivity changing the shape of a body. In the wild, an orca spends much of its time in the deep ocean, swimming up to 100 miles in a day. The external force of water keeps the fin upright. In captivity the orca spends most of its life at the water's surface, either immobile or swimming in repetitive circles. Gravity pulls the fin down so it often flops over. The lack of movement affects the shape of the orca's body as well as its mental health.[28]

Our lifestyles are changing our bodies and minds in much the same way.

Notice how many people have rounded shoulders and weak upper bodies from hours spent hunched over a computer. Sore knees, hips, and backs from years spent sitting in chairs. Inflexible ankles from a lifetime of wearing shoes.

There's even a new epidemic called "text neck" caused by hours of looking at your phone.

The human head weighs about 12 pounds. When you bend it forward and down, the weight on the spine increases to as much as 60 pounds. That's like having an eight year old hanging from your neck.[29]

Not only does this put undo pressure on your spine, it impacts your mental and emotional well-being.

Social scientist, and author, Amy Cuddy demonstrates in her TED Talk how your body posture is either enhancing or limiting your ability to express your true self.[30]

When animals feel powerful, they get bigger. You're the same. You stand tall, lift your chest and take up more space. Look at athletes who've just won a competition. They throw their arms out wide. They beam.

You also stand like this when you see someone you love and you hold your arms out to hug them. When you're in this position your chest is open and your heart feels exposed. Just watch people reuniting at an airport. Love is powerful and that feeling moves you in powerful ways.

I invite you to try it for yourself right now.

Move in a way that makes you take up more space. Imagine you see someone you love. Open your chest. Expose your heart. Look forward. Hold that position for two minutes. Then notice how you feel.

When you feel powerless the opposite happens. You look down and take up less space. You curl in on yourself, bringing your arms close in. Your heart is hidden and protected.

Think of a team that has just lost a big game. They're deflated on the bench, like balloons with the air let out. They walk to the locker room with their heads hanging ow. They feel powerless and it shows.

You can try that now for just a second, by slumping your shoulders, dropping your head, looking down and collapsing your chest. If you were to hold this position for over two minutes you'd probably feel deflated and possibly less able to access your true boundless nature.

Yet we assume this posture over our phones, sometimes for hours.

You don't notice it happening, but your body's position affects your mind and alters your moods, which directs your behavior and shapes your life.

Movement is a simple alternative to that continuous "powerless posture."

Jon Kabat-Zin, author of Wherever You Go, There You Are, says that in meditation, our posture talks to us. "If we slump, it reflects low energy, passivity, a lack of clarity. If we sit ramrod-straight, we are tense, making too much of an effort, trying too hard."[31]

He recommends that meditators "Sit in a way that embodies dignity".

I love that. I begin my morning meditation now by reminding myself to "sit with dignity", and I immediately feel more graceful and relaxed.

Your body knows the shape of dignity.

If you tell yourself to sit with dignity right now, your body will naturally adjust, and continue to adjust until you feel more dignified. This new shape of your body will affect how you feel about yourself.

Your body knows the shape of all emotions. You can impact your emotions by how you move.

Feeling depressed, stressed, or overwhelmed? Notice the shape of your body, and move it in powerful ways for a few minutes. Then notice how you feel.

At times we all experience big emotions: fear, excitement, anger, and grief. Holding them in, and stuffing them down can create all kinds of stress. Since emotions are energy, you can free yourself of the pressure within just by directing that energy through movement. (See Release for more.)

Movement can change your destiny.

Your DNA code never changes. You may be "programmed" for disease, but your life isn't predetermined. Thousands of sequences, patterns and combinations are possible, and you can affect what you become.

Joe Dispenza, writes in You Are the Placebo, "We can modify our genetic destiny by turning on the genes we want and turning off the genes we don't want through working with the various factors in the environment that program our genes."[32]

Movement is one of those factors that can change the operation of your genes.

By paying attention to your body throughout the day, and moving in the many ways it wants to move, you'll express the life that's within your cells.

It can be as simple as taking a quick break to arch your back and stretch your arms out. You'll probably yawn as you do this, pulling more oxygen into your cells, and filling yourself up with energy.

By taking a break to move you can alter your relationship to time, reconnect with your primal nature and add a rich sensuality to your life.

Hearing the impulses of your body can take time at first.

Most of us are use to treating our bodies as slaves of the mind, as if its purpose is to get our brain from place to place. We're so disconnected from our bodies that we don't even know what our authentic movement would be. We don't feel the impulses within.

Even if you exercise regularly, it's possible to be disconnected from your body's wisdom with ideas about how you should look and perform.

It's not uncommon to push yourself mentally while you sit at your desk all day and then push yourself physically when you work out, always in a state of doing, but overall moving very little. If you exercise you may think your life isn't sedentary, but even if you workout an hour each day, you're likely to be inactive as much as 14 hours a day.

In those non-exercising hours there are hundreds of opportunities to move in ways that connect you to your body, and don't get in the way of getting stuff done. In fact, it will just make getting stuff done much more pleasurable.

It's easy to lose awareness of your body by relating to life through your thoughts. This metaphor may help you feel the different experience that's possible when you allow your mind to settle into your body, so they two can live as one again.

Think of your body as a horse and your mind as the rider.

In a typical mind-driven, sedentary life, the rider takes the horse out of its stall where it's been all night. The rider jumps on the horse and takes off in a straight line to get to destinations in the quickest way possible. She spurs and whips the horse to keep it going at maximum speed. At times the rider strains up out of the saddle leaning over the horse's neck, willing it to run faster. Though the horse gallops at a breakneck pace, the two are at odds. The rider arrives at her destination tense and sore. The horse is depleted.

After taking the rider where she needs to go, the horse is kept in a small pen until the rider needs it again.

The horse develops ailments from running at full speed and being inactive the rest of the time. The rider begrudges the vet bills and down time. She eases up on the pressure when the horse is recovering, but returns to full pace when it has healed.

But there's a different way to be. You still get where you need to go, but you can do it with more connection, rhythm, and grace.

In this new scenario, the rider takes a moment to pet the horse and connect with it, allowing it to move after being in its stall for hours. The rider climbs on to the horse, letting go of tension as she settles into the saddle, letting the strong beast take all of her weight. Her relaxed thighs rest on the horse's middle. She feels its ribs expand and contract with each breath.

Through slight hand movements, shifting her weight, and squeezing her thighs, she guides the horse to change direction and speed, always feeling the horse beneath her. The two move as one gracefully. The rider takes a route with hills and valleys, flat plains and streams to cross, knowing the journey is as important as the destination. At times she lets the horse guide, since it knows the way to go. She gets to her destination relaxed and enlivened.

Once there, she lets the horse out in a field where it will walk, run, be still, toss its head like a rock star, chase other horses, and roll in the dust.

In this way the rider values the horse and its service. After years of being together, the rider senses the horse's mood in little time, just as the horse can sense the rider.

Your mind and body aren't separate, like a horse and rider, yet we often act as if they are. When you allow your mind to let go of its tight grip on the reigns, and trust the instincts and impulses of your body, you'll realize a range of movement and sensation you hadn't noticed before. You'll feel freer, stronger, and more capable. You'll reconnect the sense of mind and body as one.

You'll discover your own natural rhythm and pace, and be fueled by the pulse of wellbeing. A more primal, instinctual wisdom within you will emerge. Your truth will become clearer. Decisions will become easier.

You'll become truly comfortable in your own skin.

Why is it so hard to get moving?

A simple answer comes from classical physics. Inertia: An object at rest will stay at rest until something influences it.

The hardest part about moving can be the force it takes to get off the couch.

The good news is that once you get going, inertia, which works against you when you're stationary, works in your favor when you move. An object in motion will stay in motion until something influences it.

Most of the fuel it takes to send a spaceship to the moon is burned getting out of the earth's gravitational pull. The same is true for you.

To get through the force and overcome inertia you may have to will yourself to move. Getting your butt out of the chair may be the hardest part, but once you're up and moving, it gets much easier.

Living a primarily sedentary life isn't natural.

It's become a habit over decades. Most of this was conditioned before you could decide for yourself. Your feet were put into shoes. You were pushed around in a carriage. You sat in school, learned to drive, and probably spent many hours in front of a screen.

Habits are behaviors that you do automatically, without thinking about them. But you learned them over a long time.

Make movement a habit.

If you want to know the power of expressing your true self, experience more pleasure in your body, and have more connection to your wisdom and creativity, it's time to making authentic movement a habit.

You probably think you make choices more than you actually do. You live a big chunk of your life by unconscious habits. You have to operate this way, otherwise you'd be overwhelmed by the thousands of choices you have to make each day.

Many of these habits override your body's desires, natural rhythm, and wisdom.

Your day may look something like this: You get out of bed, grab a coffee, exercise, shower, dress, eat breakfast, check your phone, and get to work, without paying much attention to how your body feels.

Your head drives the agenda and sets the pace, like that first rider and horse in the example above.

To move in ways that are natural and authentic you'll have to become aware of what you're sensing in your body. You'll be tempted to move in ways you've been taught, and ways you think look good.

Your body doesn't care about what looks good. Your body wants what feels good. So if you want to feel good, listen to what your body wants, and do that.

To become of aware of your body's impulses you need only pay attention. When you pay attention, you become present. Presence brings to consciousness what has been unconscious in you.

Find your groove.

My main groove is dancing, as you may have guessed from the story above. It's always been a quick route for me to connect with myself.

I'll close my eyes and get lost in the rhythm and flow of music. Whether it's slow and sultry, bright and twangy, or raucous and angry, my body responds with fleshly pleasure. I lose my sense of identity and feel my true self when I'm dancing. Not every single time I dance, but often.

Dancing isn't my only groove. There are lots of ways my body likes to move. If you haven't found your groove yet, don't worry. If you'll experiment and explore different ways to move, you'll eventually find the ways that are truly yours. At first it may take some effort.

If your body is used to being sedentary, it may resist waking up.

Keep trying different things until you find what moves you. Sometimes moving in new ways is unpleasant. It can be uncomfortable to do new things, but variety of movement is enlivening. Your brain has to figure out new ways to get things done. It builds new pathways to accomplish new movements. New movements keep your brain fit.

When you allow your body to move the ways it wants, you'll discover your natural rhythm, and a grace in your system that is yours alone. You'll experience the pleasure of your own pace, full of variations.

That pleasure will be a conduit to your true self and your authentic power.

I'd been a very active adult, exercising regularly, cycling to work, always in motion, but most of the time I was moving in a way that was actually overriding my body's wisdom. I had to learn to live in sync with myself.

For me, learning how to move authentically began by slowing down.

I was fortunate enough to study Continuum Movement with the founder, Emilie Conrad. She developed this practice of feeling the smallest of impulses in your body, and following them through their natural unfolding.

Emilie was smart and articulate and could discourse at great length about her political view, but when she practiced Continuum she was the most fluid and graceful human I'd ever seen. Her body exuded an intelligence that seemed free of constrictions. Emilie was in her 70s when I studied with her.[33]

In her class I would slow down and notice what my body wanted to do. With eyes closed I might feel a finger wanting to straighten, which could lead to a slow twist of the wrist. That impulse could snake through my body, opening my mouth, unfurling my tongue and tilting my head back in unusual ways.

Following the subtlest sensations, my tight muscles would often unwind effortlessly. My mind thought it knew how I should move, but every time I heard thoughts about what I should do, I would breathe and feel what my body wanted to do instead.

I always left class with an expanded sense of myself. I stood taller, feeling more space in my chest. My arms swung easily by my sides and my steps were more graceful.

During class and afterwards, I experienced great insights into issues in my life.

Simply by slowing down, and paying attention you can connect with yourself in a profound way. This can heal your body and soul, and guide your life.

Find your tribe.

My mom was my original tribe, in every way, including dance.

Every morning before school she'd turn on the radio and we'd dance. It would never have occurred to me to start my day that way. Sometimes moms really do know best. Together we'd shimmy and shake and laugh. It was a joyful way to connect with myself and with her, before shuffling off to the drudgery at school.

Though I never took a dance class, dancing became a way of life. And that led me to more of my tribe.

Several decades after those mornings with my mom I was dancing with my eyes closed, swept up in the pleasure when I met my husband. He danced up to me and together we swayed, dipped, and twirled for over an hour before we ever spoke a word. Fourteen years later we're still dancing through life together.

It's a simple way for us to connect without words.

I still love to dance alone, with my eyes closed, as a way to connect with the divine consciousness that is my true self, but there's something enlivening about dancing with others. Whether it's kicking up our heels at a wedding, or taking a 5 Rhythms class near my home, engaging with others through movement is a primal and pleasurable way to connect

If you're having trouble getting off the couch, find a buddy. Whether it's just one other person or a whole group, research shows that most people enjoy physical activity more when they do it with others, and when they have a good time they're more likely to continue.[26]

If you think you'd like to walk more, run more, surf or stretch more, make a date with a friend. Take a lesson, or join a club. You can find walking clubs, running groups, rock climbing classes and ecstatic dance tribes. Check them out and see what appeals to you. Adding movement to your life can be a great way to expand your relationships.

Making a commitment to others will get you started.

Give everything more than just one try. Remember, learning can be uncomfortable. Movement feels better the more you do it.

If you can't find a tribe, don't let it stop you. I just recommend it as a way to help you get going. I love doing yoga, taking beach walks, and exercising by myself. That time alone to connect with my body and feel its rhythm is precious to me in a way that is different from the connection I get with others.

If you really want to get the most out of movement, take it outside.

We humans spend far more time indoors then we're meant to. This disconnection from the natural world also disconnects us from our own true nature, and is the cause of many of our mental and physical ailments.

Research shows that time in nature has real and measurable benefits to your physical and emotional wellbeing. It reduces stress, anxiety, and aggression. It improves your recovery time, mental focus and sense of connection.

Alan Logan, ND, co-author of Your Brain on Nature says, "Green exercise is like exercise squared. We know that exercise is good for us and that being outside is good for us, but when combined, their benefits are even greater."[34]

I learned to incorporate natural movement into work from Joel Solomon, the President of the venture capital firm where I used to work. He taught me to start business gatherings with yoga, singing, and poetry. End them with dancing and drumming. And whenever possible, have them outside.

Moving together has a way of leveling the playing field and disrupting hierarchies. It shakes up the energy, fuels creativity and improves focus. Moving in ways that are collaborative and fun creates connection. That helps bring out the best in people.

We get so few chances to move in our corporate lives, but doing so could really give you the competitive edge.

Our office had a typical boardroom with a big table and many chairs, but when we had things to discuss Joel and I would often go outside. Walking along the seawall with the mountains to our side, we'd talk about opportunities, our current businesses, and how to support our CEOs.

Being in movement, side by side, outdoors, shaped our conversations and connection, as much as the words we spoke.

When you move authentically your relationship to your body changes. You come to accept it as it is. Movement will help you love your body, even as it reshapes and changes you.

To move through the inertia of sedentary living to a life full of authentic movement, start with small steps.

Add some movement to what you regularly do.

In the practice section I'll give you some specific ways to add movement to your life. It's best to keep it really simple, and fit it into what you're already doing.

Before you jump out of bed, just breathe and stretch, and notice how you feel. Spend a few seconds moving your body in ways that feel good.

Get off the elevator one stop early and take the stairs that last flight up or down. Park your car further away than you normally would, and walk the extra distance. Your body is designed to walk and climb.

Move your laptop to a counter and work standing up for part of your day. Get up and go talk to someone in the office instead of sending an email. Walk or cycle to do your errands.

Watch TV from the floor. When you're not held in place by the couch you'll sense your body more. You'll move around to get comfortable. Roll, stretch, and squat while you're down there.

Dance while you're cooking. Squat while brushing your teeth. Crouch and stretch when you watch your kids play soccer. Take a walk with your friend when you meet for coffee.

When clients are stuck and know they need to move more, I invite them to start by setting a timer to ring several times a day. The ring reminds them to move. For some, it isn't until they stretch and take a deep breath that they feel the strain of being hunched over their keyboard for hours.

Moving their body makes them aware of how they feel.

Some fear the interruption of an alarm, and some find it irritating at first, but it can be difficult to create a new habit without a reminder. Those who use the alarm report returning to their work refreshed, happier, energized and better able to focus, after just a few minutes of moving around.

As a florist, Joan was either standing for hours, creating floral arrangements, or sitting for hours, doing paperwork. Between getting her kids ready for school in the morning, making dinner, helping with homework and getting them to bed at night, she had no time left for exercise.

She used to go to the gym regularly, and she knew that working out would make her feel better, but the effort to get started was more than she could muster. Rather than add more stress by trying to fit a workout into her busy days we added movement to what she was already doing.

Joan asked her 11 year old to create a playlist of songs from the 70s. She played it at work and started dancing while making arrangements. It energized her. She found herself smiling more. She was getting her work done in a whole new way.

Joan invited her two part time employees to bring in playlists of their own. They became the dancing florists. When she worked back in her office, Joan set an alarm for every hour. When it rang she would get up and stretch and breathe deeply. For 5 minutes she moved in ways that felt good. Then she'd return to her work. She found these breaks helped her focus on work more effectively.

It's common to think it's more efficient to plow through work. By leading with your mind and just focusing on getting things done, you can accomplish results, but you'll miss out on the many pleasurable sensations, wisdom and guidance from your body. By allowing for pleasure you may be amazed at how much more you accomplish.

The habit followed Joan home. She initiated breaks when helping her daughters study. She often played music in the kitchen while preparing dinner. Moving throughout the day, turned into moving more at night, which led to moving more on her days off.

In good weather she began riding her bike to the shop. The more she moved, the more energy she felt. The more energy she felt, the more she moved. She felt better in her body. This improved her mood and her confidence. She met a man who got her running, hiking, and falling in love.

Movement is vital for your health. It strengthens your body and mind. It can fill your day, boost your mood, enrich your relations and fulfill your soul. By paying attention to your impulses and moving authentically you can realize your authentic self, beyond all the ideas about who you should be.

Here are simple ways to get moving.

MOVE

Practices

– ADD MOVEMENT –

This is a simple way to add movement to what you're doing, and stay connected to your body.

Add more movement to what you already do.

 Pick one thing you do every single day. Brush your teeth, make phone calls, sit down, stand up, etc.

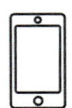 Add one new movement to that action, every time you do it.
It might look like this:

You walk around whenever you make a phone call, do jumping jacks while you wait for your coffee to brew, dance as you brush your teeth.

 Just move every time you do that one thing.

 Notice how you feel when you're moving, and how you feel after you move.

Keep it simple. You might stretch whenever you stand up, or every morning when you get out of bed. It doesn't have to be a whole yoga routine, just a stretch that feels good.

After you've been adding movement to one thing you regularly do for long enough that it's become a habit, you can add it to more things.

Just add one thing at a time. It's better to be minimal and consistent, than go all out and burn out. Be creative. Make it fun. Follow the pleasure.

– SET AN ALARM TO MOVE –

When forming a new habit, reminders can make all the difference.

 Decide how many times you want to take a movement break.

 Set your alarm to ring at those times during the day.

 When your alarm rings, take a breath and move your body in any way that feels good.

 Notice how you feel after you move.

When the alarm rings you can get up and move around. If you're driving or in a meeting and can't get up, you can roll your shoulders, adjust your seat, wiggle your toes, take a deep breath and sit with dignity.

It is better to commit to less movement and accomplish it, than set a huge goal that you can't achieve. Start with two or three times a day. Even start with one. That will add more movement than you're getting now.

– COMMIT TO MOVE EVERY SINGLE DAY –

Getting over the inertia of a sedentary life can take effort. By committing to simple, doable movements, and tracking your progress, you can bring movement into your life bit by bit.

 Pick some form of movement you'd like to do every single day.

 Pick a minimum amount of time, or distance, or repetitions that you'll do.

 Make a commitment to do it every single day, no matter what, for at least 30 days.

 Record your progress every day.

Maybe you'd like to walk 5 miles a day, or do half an hour of yoga. Can you commit to doing that every single day?

If not, break that down to something simpler. Can you walk around your block as a minimum each day or do 4 asanas every morning?

When you commit to the minimum, you make it easy to be successful.

You can always do more than the minimum if you like. Once you get moving, more movement will be easier.

Tracking your progress in a journal or calendar will increase your sense of pleasure and help keep you motivated.

– COMMIT TO A TRIBE –

If you're having trouble moving the way you'd like, connect with others and move together.

 If there's a physical activity you like, used to do, or would like to start, find a person or group to do it with.

 Make a commitment to show up for them and for yourself.

 Commit to the minimum you know you can do. You may just commit to meeting once to start. Over committing can lead to overwhelm, and after an enthusiastic start, you'll give up.

 Add more as you experience the benefits. Pick a minimum amount of time, or distance, or repetitions that you'll do.

If you can't connect with a physical tribe you may be able to join a tribe online to help stay motivated.

Have a conference call with friends once a week. Each of you commits to the movement you're going to do. Then report back when you've done it. Talk about your successes, challenges and experiences and help each other stay inspired.

If you've got a friend who lives far away, talk on your cell phone while you take long walks.

– TRY SOMETHING NEW –

Since your body is capable of moving in a wide variety of ways, you'll benefit from trying different ways of moving.

 Commit to moving in a new way every week.

 Keep it as simple as possible. (It can be walking backwards, walking like a crab, rolling down a hill, playing hopscotch, paddle-boarding, playing soccer with your kids, jumping on a trampoline)

 Do it once during the week, or every day for a week.

 Record your progress to track the different moves you try.

Moving in new ways will engage different parts of your body, create new pathways in your brain, and enhance your moods. Tracking it will increase your dopamine, increasing your sense of pleasure and motivation.

– Feel your Body's Impulse to Move –

Go to: www.debrajoy.me/practices for a guided meditation to follow your body's impulses

This guided meditation will help you feel your body's impulses to move. As you allow your authentic movements to guide you, you'll develop a more intimate relationship with your body's wisdom.

You'll notice how often your mind interrupts your body's movement with ideas of how and where you should move.

In this practice I'll gently guide you back, over and over again to feeling your body's authentic desires beneath your mind's ideas of what you should do.

This is one of the few practices that doesn't fit into what you're already doing in your day, but if you want to explore authentic movement a little deeper this can really be a sensuous and pleasurable ride.

– YOUR PRACTICE –

WHAT:

_____

Name this practice

WHY:

_____

_____

What do you expect to gain from this practice?
Knowing why you're doing it will help keep you motivated.

BREAK YOUR PRACTICE DOWN INTO VERY SIMPLE STEPS.

1. _____

   _____

2. _____

   _____

3. _____

   _____

4. _____

   _____

TRIGGER:

_____

When developing a new habit it's best to do it every day, at the same time if possible, and it's
important to have something that reminds you, or triggers you to do it.

What will trigger you to do this practice?

- NOTES -

RELEASE

This being human is a guest house.
Every morning a new arrival.
A joy, a depression, a meanness,
some momentary awareness comes
as an unexpected visitor.

Welcome and entertain them all!
Even if they're a crowd of sorrows,
who violently sweep your house
empty of its furniture,
still treat each guest honorably.
He may be clearing you out
for some new delight.

The dark thought, the shame, the malice,
meet them at the door laughing,
and invite them in.

Be grateful for whoever comes,
because each has been sent
as a guide from beyond.
~ Rumi

This poem by Rumi is a rather long quote to open this chapter, but I could think of no better way to describe the relationship with emotions that will truly set you free.

You know how it feels when you let yourself cry.

Tears stream down your face and your nose runs. You gasp for air and suck in deep breaths. Your belly contracts with sobs that could morph into laughter at any moment. As your body calms down, your breathing softens. You exhale deeply. You feel tired but more relaxed, as if you've just done an intense workout.

Even if you collapse afterwards, you feel somehow lighter for having let it go.

There's a reason it's called "having a good cry."

Though you may feel wiped out immediately after a big release like this, over time you feel more energized and alive when you allow the energy to flow. The movement clears you out, making space for something new.

You feel fresher, like air after an electrical storm.

From the description of the good cry it's easy to imagine an emotion that triggered all that release, but we don't actually know what caused it. It could be the burning tears of a heart-wrenching breakup or the rush of joy and pride from winning an Olympic gold medal. All we know is that something was sensed and expressed.

What's the difference between sensations and emotions?

Sensations are physical feelings in your body: hot, cold, sharp, tight, stiff, fluttering, tingling, softening.

Emotions are the meaning you give those feelings: anxious, sad, excited, irritated, happy, scared.

Your physical sensations happen in the moment. One is not necessarily better than another. They just are what they are. The meaning you give them is based on your past experience, culture, and conditioning.[46]

So when I feel hot and sweaty, my heart is racing and I'm gasping for air, I might feel scared because I'm about to go on stage in front of a large group, I might be excited because I'm riding a roller coaster, or ecstatic because I'm having sex.

While the sensations may be similar, the context, (whether I'm in a bedroom with a lover or an auditorium with strangers), my history (I hate public speaking, and love roller coasters), and my culture (most people in my circle agree that public speaking is scary and orgasms are great), will determine my emotion.

Why am I telling you all this?

Emotions are energy and energy moves.

The root of the word emotion comes from the Latin "emovere", meaning "to move out or remove". If you'll feel the sensations and allow them to do what's natural, you'll find that they move quickly, and the emotion moves along with it.

Unfortunately we don't treat emotions as energy.

Rather than experience them and let them go, you might analyze them, fear them, discuss them, deny them, or try to hold onto them.

When you say, "I'm furious", "I'm depressed", or "I'm happy", you're not actually describing yourself, but the meaning you're giving your experience. But emotions can become a way that you define yourself.

When you identify with your emotions and you lose yourself in them, you have all sorts of thoughts about them and about yourself. When that happens it's easy to lose touch with the subtle energetic shifts within that are in constant flow. You lose some connection to the expression of life inside you.

Why does this matter?

Identifying with your emotions can create a false self, based on a story, and that can keep you from knowing your true self. Sensations can be a way out of the story and identity that keeps you stuck.

When you become aware of the sensations in your body that are transforming into something new all the time, you can also realize that you're not those ever-changing sensations. You're more than just aware of them. You may discover that you're awareness itself, the divine energy in which these sensations exist.

You might like some sensations more than others, but when you experience them without giving them meaning, you're not going to hold on to them. You'll allow them and let them be. This can set you free.

Sensations are like champagne bubbles.

The effervescence is what makes champagne special. The tiny

bubbles seem to appear out of nothing at the bottom of your glass, race to the surface, and vanish. They live short but energetic lives.

Though the bubbles seem to disappear, the energy actually transmutes. The bubbles explode when they reach the surface, creating a tiny crater. The crater closes, ejecting a thin thread of liquid that breaks up into tiny droplets that fly through the air. That's why you'll get bubbles up your nose when you take a sip.

Champagne bubbles aren't good or bad. They're just energy.

When you watch bubbles rise in your glass, and feel them on your skin, you probably don't judge them. You don't think, "These bubbles are good. Those ones are bad." You don't try to stop some, and encourage others. You probably watch, taste and feel.

You can do the same with your physical sensations, and stop judging how you feel. When you don't get attached to feelings, or try to deny them, your emotions will no longer define you or control you.

Implicitly or explicitly you were told how you should feel.

At an early age you learned which emotions were good to have and which were bad, and so the judgments you have about them today may not even be your own. You probably formed them before you could decide for yourself.

If your family valued humility, they may have warned you not to get too big for your britches. Now guilt squelches the joy you feel when you do something great.

Perhaps your loving parents said, "don't cry" as they comforted you, and now you choke back your tears automatically.

You may have grown up in a family where lust was considered a sin so you suppress sexual energy when it stirs inside you, even though it's as natural as feeling hunger or thirst.

It could be something as subtle as a teacher shushing you when you shouted in play, or being punished for having a tantrum. At some point you were likely coaxed, coerced, or cajoled into suppressing your authentic feelings, by a parent, teacher, sibling, or friend.

Through all the messages you got about your feelings, you quickly figured out what was acceptable to your tribe. We're social animals. We need to be accepted. And we'll do what we have to do to fit in.

You allow the feelings that are socially acceptable and deny the ones that aren't.

To stop your feelings from moving as they naturally do, you might have clenched your jaw, tightened your belly, or held your breath. Though you did this consciously at first as a kid, to stop from feeling, over the years these reactions to sensations and emotions became immediate and automatic. Now it's probably happening without you even knowing. And that creates chronic tension in your body and mind.

Though this saved you from feeling the sensations and emotions you weren't supposed to feel, it didn't make them go away. The tingling, bubbling, burning, and softening, the excitement, fear, desire, and pain that could have dispersed in seconds if they'd been allowed, got trapped. That energy is still looking for an escape.

Rather than being a vessel for energies to flow through, your body became a holding tank, and the pressure continues to grow. Think of a champagne bottle with 10 million bubbles pushing against the cork.

Something sets you off and the energy blasts through.

You rage at the driver ahead of you, who slows down unexpectedly. You yell at your kid for spilling juice, sob uncontrollably at a commercial, or laugh hysterically and can't stop.

When energy explodes like this, whether it's extreme anger, fear, or even joy, it can shock others and embarrass you. In some cases, people can get hurt.

After an instant of relief in your body, you might feel uneasy, even ashamed, about what just came out of you. That can re-enforce the idea that your physical sensations and emotions are wrong, and even dangerous. It feels safer to keep them under wraps again.

It takes a lot of your unconscious effort to keep that energy in.

We don't all have big emotions building up this way, but we all have energies running through us that we suppress.

Think of feelings running through your body like water running through a hose.

If you hold a garden hose in your hand and turn on the faucet, the water will flow through. You can easily stop the water just by twisting the hose, but once you've clamped down on that hose you have to hold it tight to keep the water in.

As long as you keep the hose kinked, water pressure builds up behind your hand.

You know what happens when you try to stop laughing.

You clamp your jaw shut, or bite the inside of your cheek. You cover your mouth and still the laughter escapes ... through your nose. It turns into tears. The harder you try to stop, the harder you laugh.

Have you ever felt like crying, but held it in?

You get that uncomfortable lump in your throat. Your muscles tighten. It can lead to a headache.

Though you're much more sophisticated and complicated than a garden hose, as you try to hold down energy, you create all sorts of kinks in your system, and the pressure builds. If you release your grip for just a second the energy comes gushing out. It may not have the force of champagne popping, but it can be stronger than you want.

When you try to hold feelings in it not only sucks your energy, it can lead to heavy moods that last for hours, days, or more.

What could have been cleared in a few seconds or minutes becomes lingering frustration, irritability, lethargy, or anxiety. Over years it can lead to depression, aches and pains, and even disease.

The energy won't always escape in big ways, but it will escape.

When the outlet is blocked, water will drip through the smallest hole in a garden hose to relieve pressure. The energy of your emotions will do the same.

Your unexpressed childhood rage may seep out through your voice, as a bitter tone you don't hear. The heaviness of your un-cried tears hovers like a dark cloud. Your light-hearted laughter and happiness find outlets only when you're drinking and let down your guard.

You may not even notice it's happening, but no doubt others will.

We're all energetic beings. We sense energy, and respond to it.

It's that creepy feeling you get that stops you from walking down a certain street. It's what told you to say yes to an opportunity, when rationale would have you say no. It makes you want to come closer to a person and get to know him better, or stay away.

When you're unaware of energy seeping out, relationships can be confusing and challenging. Feelings are authentic and natural. When you deny them, and try to hide them from yourself and others, people sense that you're not being completely authentic. They may not know what it is, but they'll know that something's not right. They may not trust you completely, even if they're not sure why.

This can leave you feeling hurt and misunderstood.

All the while you're just trying to be who you thought you were suppose to be. It's a way to protect yourself, but you can end up feeling empty and alone.

The idea of who you're supposed to be can never match the fullness of who you really are.

Psychotherapist Carl Jung said that the primitive emotions and impulses we don't acknowledge in ourselves become a shadow.[47]

What you haven't accepted about yourself, you'll stuff into the darkness of your unconscious. Trying to hide aspects of your humanity keeps you firmly ensconced in an identity of who you think you should be.[48]

You'll see this sometimes in people who've found spirituality or personal growth as an escape from being an ordinary human with needs and flaws. They've discovered an ideal of how to be that may be admirable, but it's rarely attainable.

Rather than continue on a path of wholeness with all its imperfections, they deny the parts of themselves that don't fit the image of who they think they should be. They genuinely want to be compassionate, accepting, and peacefully walking a sacred path. Any feelings that don't fit that identity get suppressed, but they can't be held down forever.

Energy can be transmuted, but it can't be destroyed.

You might see this energy in the yogi who desperately wants peace, unaware that she has a death grip on her steering wheel and is clenching her teeth when she's late for class.

It's the sexual urges that the celibate seeker stuffs down with cupcakes and cookies, trying to fill up with external pleasures and numb internal sensations.

It's the corporate executive who wants to take on more work and avoids the ulcer that's telling him something's wrong.

While they may believe they're rid of the feelings they no longer want to have, energy always finds its release, sometimes in strange and confusing ways.

I tried for years to suppress my big emotions.

My mom was the queen of fun. After dancing in the living room, we'd sing out loud to pop songs as she drove me to school. But school didn't allow for the joy I felt inside. I squelched my laughter, believing I was too loud. I stuffed down my feelings. I felt stupid and slow.

My mom had to work several jobs after my dad left us. I didn't want to add to her burdens, so I numbed my loneliness and boredom with television when she worked late at night.

Whenever adults cried they always apologized, so I held in my own tears, thinking it made me more grown up.

It was only in my adult years that I learned to sense the full range of my authentic feelings again. Even the ones I didn't want to feel. Over the years I experienced my emotions by listening to the signals of my body, the way one might listen at the feet of a guru.

I've swallowed my pride and dropped my identity as someone who "keeps it together." I've been willing to be too loud, too joyful, too sad, and altogether too much, by letting the energies flow.

I dance in the morning just because I feel good. I sing out loud. I skip down the road. When my dog died I sobbed and allowed myself to feel all the pain of the loss, and the hugeness of the love as I walked the streets without him. Even now, years after his death, I can think of him and cry. I just let the tears flow.

It's taken me years to just let my feelings be.

It all started with regular deep breathing and grounding. Over time, that got me out of my chronic thinking and into sensing my body. Once I was able to experience my internal sensations, it took practice to not override them, ignore them, and hope they'd go away.

Feelings aren't always convenient, and they aren't always comfortable, but I learned that if I kept coming back to the sensations in gentle ways, it got easier. I'd feel them and notice how they changed. I'd express them in private and notice how I felt.

I still make mistakes.

I override my body's wisdom and find myself in old patterns of stuffing feelings down. But the moment I become aware and allow them to move, I feel free. I've found it's never too late.

You can't deny some feelings without denying others.

When you cut yourself off from feeling some of the painful emotions you're holding in your body, you also miss feeling some of the pleasures inside.

At some point we all push down feelings and suppress aspects of ourselves. There are times when keeping things to yourself is appropriate. Part of living in community is taking one another's needs into consideration. Occasionally holding back makes it easier to get along. Expressing yourself fully in the moment may not always be safe.

But when you continually deny a part of yourself because somewhere in your life you got the idea that it was bad, you may be inadvertently suppressing aspects of your own joy, creativity and passion as well. You're dampening your own life force.

Let's say you were raised to believe that anger is bad, or you grew up afraid of it, like I did. You wouldn't want to feel it in yourself, and you wouldn't want to hurt others with it.

When sensations arise that you associate with anger - heat, tingling, pressure, or contraction—you may want to escape those feelings. Focusing your attention away from your body would seem to be the simplest way. By avoiding the feelings, they seem to disappear.

All of this would happen unconsciously and automatically, but it could lead to living mostly through your thoughts, denying your body, and missing out on a world of pleasures.

Denying your sensations of anger, sadness, fear, joy, or whichever feelings you might avoid, you'll deny other feelings as well.

Being angry, sad, turned on, wildly ecstatic, and afraid, are all a part of being human. You can try to control these energies, but it's their nature to transmute.

Until you allow the sensations within you to be experienced without judgment, you'll never accept yourself completely. If you can't accept yourself, you can't fully accept others, and you can't accept life as it is.

Without acceptance, you'll constantly be in resistance. You can never truly know peace. Without acceptance, you'll never experience your true power.

Allowing the feelings you don't want, frees up more of the feelings you do want.

When I was little, my biological dad wasn't around very much, but when he was he made a big impression. He was explosive. Our family would be having a lovely time and something would set him off – BOOM - he'd rage.

He never hit us, but his screaming tirades had me fearing for my life.

Living with that uncertainty can traumatize a kid. Though he didn't live with us for long, my fear of anger lasted for decades.

When I was dealing with debilitating illness in my thirties, my acupuncturist told me that my liver was "pushy." He kept gently explaining that in Traditional Chinese Medicine the liver represents anger. I could admit that I was angry about environmental destruction, cruelty to animals, and other injustices in the world, but he was trying to nudge me towards something more primal and personal. Try as I did, I just couldn't feel it.

It wasn't until some years later that I felt an explosive energy rise up in me.

I was in a therapist's office. He skillfully created a safe space for me to express it. The impulse was so powerful that I began to punch and roar like a wild beast. His place was well equipped to allow all of it, all of me, without anyone getting hurt. It was the force of someone fighting for her life.

If you'd seen me beating and howling, you'd say I was enraged. But more than anything else, I was enlivened.

I'd been unconsciously using my life force to hold this energy down for decades.

By letting the energy move through me the moment I sensed it, I could feel its power. That power was mine, but it was bigger than me. It was flowing through me and all I had to do was allow it.

It wasn't the kind of blind rage you hear about where people don't know what they're doing.

I was completely aware, noticing the impulse rise up and consciously allowing it to move through me. I could stop at any time, but I knew it had to be released.

Though roaring and punching furiously, I wasn't angry about anything in particular. There was no story that accompanied this outburst. No face I was seeing as I punched and screamed. It was just pure energy rushing through me.

It was only a fraction of the emotions I'd pushed down for decades. It was the primal energy my acupuncturist had been pointing to so many years ago.

When thoroughly exhausted, I collapsed on the floor, and began to laugh...and laugh... and laugh. Elation had been trapped behind that geyser of energy.

Releasing anger can open the door to more joy inside.

Like an animal that shakes off the energy after a fight, I felt free. I had let it go.

That wasn't the end of anger for me, but it was the beginning of freedom from holding it in. It was a pivotal moment in my life.

It was only after I began releasing anger that I could feel the fear that had been buried underneath. The more I practiced releasing my anger and fear, the more free I felt to express my joy.

Since I don't live in the soundproof safety of a therapist's office, I don't let that energy gush out any time it bubbles up. I don't go around striking out and screaming, just because I feel like it. I recommend you don't do that either.

It might sound like I spend a lot of time gushing like a fire hydrant, and who'd want to hang around that for long? But since I started releasing energy regularly, it takes no time at all. By sensing my feelings, allowing them, breathing deeply and releasing if needed, I have less anxiety and more clarity.

People say that it's easy to be around me. They feel seen and heard. They trust me. I'm not a saint, not even close. But releasing blocked energy, reduces tension and anxiety. It enables me to stay more aligned with my true self, and more present with others.

Clinging to emotions can create as much pressure as denying them.

We all have preferences for how we want to feel.

I'd rather feel excited than afraid, happy rather than sad. I acknowledge my preferences, and still try to be an equal opportunity feeler. I want to follow Rumi's advice and treat each feeling like a welcomed houseguest.

A challenge comes when you get attached to feeling a certain way.

Though it's sad to see some feelings go, you have to open the door and say goodbye when it's time. If you don't, you're just holding them hostage. That's where the struggle begins.

Good feelings need to move just like all others. When you try to hold on to a feeling, rather than just experience it, you're resisting the flow of life. That creates stress in your body and mind.

You miss out on the freshness of each new moment if you cling to the past.

Letting good feelings flow through you, and sensing them as they move, can be a challenge for all of us. You may unconsciously feel that you aren't allowed to have it too good. You may automatically dampen down your own joy. I did that many times in my life. At times I still do.

Great feelings can be overwhelming at times. The chapter Ground can help you handle more good feelings in your life in a way that is enlivening and sustainable.

Denying your feelings, or clinging to them, can trigger addictions.

You feel something you'd rather avoid, and you quickly numb the sensation with the distraction of technology, drugs, sex, food, exercise or work.

Something great happens in your life and you want to celebrate, or you just feel good and want to stay that way. You automatically have a drink, or eat junk food to keep the buzz going.

For some of us, those distractions are addictions.

With addiction, one leads to another as you try to numb the pain or maintain the high, rather than let feelings ebb and flow. Addiction overrides your natural sensations, which would guide you towards pleasure in nourishing ways.

With addiction you feel depleted. Over time you may even feel ashamed. These feelings can trigger addictions again.

Eating, drinking, exercising, shopping or throwing yourself into work when you feel good or bad, doesn't mean you've got an addiction. But if you're dealing with addiction, it's keeping you from experiencing the true pleasure that's your birthright.

Here's how emotions and addiction collided in me one day.

A few years ago I had one of those amazing days when everything was going right. I woke up feeling fantastic; happy and light, spacious inside. The weather was perfect and dolphins greeted me on my morning beach walk. My husband shared some great news with me about a project he'd been working on for years. I was so excited I could barely contain it.

I wanted to dance around and jump for joy. I often feel that way, but have developed the habit of holding it in. So after a quick happy exchange with my man, I got in the car to do errands.

While driving, I was suddenly overwhelmed with a craving for chocolate chip cookies. Not just warm, chewy, fresh baked goodness. Any crappy store-bought, (gluten-free), junk would be my fix. I wanted to gobble up a whole bag.

As soon as I noticed this craving I breathed deeply. It was uncomfortable. My skin felt too tight to expand. I was afraid I might burst. I wanted to ignore my body, speed up, and get on with my errands.

Allowing myself to breathe, even with the discomfort, slowed me down enough to become curious about this addictive monster threatening to take over my body and mind, especially when things were going so well.

Breathing slowed me down and helped me get curious. Then it hit me. This joy wanted to bubble up and out of me, and I was ignoring it, attempting to stuff it down and make it go away. I was trying to keep myself together and get on with my day, but I was like a damn about to burst.

The cookies would have numbed me to my own sensations, but they wouldn't have made the energy go away. If I'd binged the way I'd felt driven to do, it would have pushed down the huge sensations of excitement I was feeling, and left me with the pain and fatigue that sugar always brings.

So I got out of the car, planted my feet on the ground and kept breathing deeply, right there by the side of the road. I was no longer stuffing down feelings to "get on with my day." This was my day. This was my life.

Feeling my connection to the earth enabled me to let the good feelings flow through my body, without being overwhelmed. Energy was no longer surging through me as jagged excitement, the way that it had when the sugar cravings came on me. It morphed into a bold pulsation.

I felt more alive, more expanded, and more powerful. I was happy and grounded. The feelings rose through me one after the other, and I was able to handle them with ease. My body swayed very slightly, each breath like a wave.

Free of tension, I felt well the rest of the day.

It can be hard to notice old patterns because they happen automatically. But as soon as you become aware, you're no longer being ruled by unconscious habits. That's when you can choose.

If you treat your sensations like champagne bubbles, they move quickly.

You'd notice a sensation in your body that seemed to come out of nowhere. You'd feel the movement, and perhaps sense the texture weight, shape, and size.

You might even close your eyes to experience it fully, like a connoisseur, knowing it wouldn't last for long. You might become aware of other sensations, all happening at once. You'd feel the changes, and let them occur. Some feelings would intensify. Others would soften. Some would seem to disappear.

You might notice an impulse and follow its lead. By doing this you'd stay out of the drama of lingering emotions and present to the ever-changing pulse of life.

I was driving north on Lincoln Boulevard, in Venice, CA, when a big SUV heading south on the other side of the road suddenly made a sharp left turn across two solid yellow lines and into my lane. I quickly swerved to avoid being T-boned. My body's immediate response to this threat enabled me to act without thinking.

As soon as I was past the car I noticed my heart was pounding fast. I was covered in a thin film of sweat. I had gasped and was holding my breath. These were sensations - the physiological reactions of my nervous system.

When I looked in the rearview mirror and saw that big car making a wide U turn behind me I felt scared; it had almost hit me. Then angry; that MOFO could have killed me!

In a flash I was hotter. As I returned to my sensations in my body, I became aware of an impulse to let go of the gasp. I allowed it to release and exhaled deeply. A low moan came out of my mouth with the breath. My skin cooled down. I felt better and continued driving home.

My body did what it's designed to do, and it saved my life.

It would have been easy to stay stuck in an emotional state from that incident for a lot longer. Reliving in my mind what could have happened, would have amplified the sensations in my body, feeding my thoughts of fear and anger.

Instead, the fear and anger were gone as soon as I let out that moan. I returned to a sense of peace and joy immediately. I didn't think about it again, until I wrote it for this chapter.

You can start by just feeling what you feel.

There are lots of emotions you'd rather not experience, so the idea of feeling them may not be appealing.

Whether you experience happiness, jealousy, craving, excitement, anger or fear, you'll be amazed how quickly these emotions morph into something else, when you allow them.

Feeling your emotions doesn't mean you have to act on them. Sensing them is enough. It's important that you know that. You may be afraid to feel your love because you don't want to act like a fool. Fear of lashing out in a blind rage might keep you from feeling your anger.

Your emotions can be a portal to presence.

If you feel happy, ask yourself, "How do I know I'm happy?" Thoughts will rush in. "I feel good. It's sunny out." Your mind will look for reasons. That's what your mind does.

As you ask yourself how you know, see if you can notice the sensations inside you that you associate with happy. "My body feels buoyant. I have tingling in my legs. My breathing is rhythmic. My mouth feels juicy and moist. My skin feels smooth and relaxed."

It's enough to simply feel sensations in your body. Breathe and Ground so that feelings don't overwhelm you. Read those chapters for more guidance.

Whether you feel tightness, fullness, expansiveness, throbbing, bubbling, or clenching, just allow the sensations to exist. Even if you sense something uncomfortable, you'll notice it's not the only feeling. Your body is alive with a multitude of sensations.

If feeling sensations in your body is new for you, you may find yourself suddenly back up in your thoughts. That's not unusual. It happens to us all. Most of us have been trained to live up in our minds, so it's habitual to go there.

If thoughts rush in with judgments about what you're feeling, or some other random story of distraction, just bring your attention back into your body, and feel again, if you can. If you can't, that's perfectly okay. Don't try to be perfect. Just stay with the experience wherever it takes you.

Sensations and emotions are just a part of being human. When you experience yourself as present awareness, noticing the sensations inside your body, you're no longer at risk of acting out blindly.

You'll bring consciousness to new aspects of your life. In this state you can choose to respond. That choice will come from your own inner wisdom, rather than conditioned reaction.

The more you experience emotions in this dynamic way, the more you'll experience the underlying peace of your true essence.

Your essence is the same energy that beats your heart, gives birds flight, and moves the planets. It is ever present.

- When you fall in love, watch your child sleep, or eat a great meal, it's there.

- When the stock-market crashes, or your lover dies, it's there.

- When you're lying on the floor wracked in pain, not knowing if it will ever end, it's there.

It's vast enough to allow all these experiences. If you haven't accessed this core through deep breathing, meditation or whatever spiritual practice you have, you may discover it when blocked sensations get out of the way.

When you feel strong sensations you may need to move.

Paying attention to sensations is the place to start. And for most feelings, just noticing will be enough.

But there will be times when the energy inside you needs to be expressed, and you feel an impulse to move.

When faced with great stress, your body responds immediately. Your body is ready to rumble or run. This increases your heart rate, blood pressure, and energy supply. Blood rushes to your arms and legs where you'll need the strength most. (Like it did for me when the SUV almost hit me.)

Even good stress, (eustress) heightens your sense of arousal, and energizes you. This all happens automatically, before you can think about it.

By fighting or running your way out of danger, accomplishing something challenging, or expressing the burst of energy in some way, you burn through the stress hormones, as you're designed to do. When you can act on it like that, your biological stress response strengthens you, and leaves you feeling more peaceful.

That could have happened for me if I'd done my exuberant happy dance, when my husband shared his good news. Instead I stuffed down the impulse, and craved cookies later.

Now when I sense energy inside, whether it's an exuberance of joy, the heat of anger, or weight of sadness, I first accept it in my body. I don't always succeed, but that's what I'm going for. Through practice, I've learned to pay attention, and allow it to morph rather than deny or suppress it, as I used to. If that's not enough, I move with the energy as soon as I can.

I always feel lighter and more energized when I let sensations and emotions move. You will too. Maybe not at first, but if you stick with it, you'll be amazed at how free you can be.

While I was writing this chapter, I received this text from a friend, about her three year old daughter. "Sarah was upset because she didn't want to do what she'd been told. She went up to her room, shut the door and turned on her Free To Be You And ME cd. She scrolled through the songs until she got to It's Alright to Cry, and played it full blast. She wailed along with it. When she was finished she was in a fabulous, cheery mood, and we all went along as if nothing had happened."

By going somewhere private and allowing her big feelings to flow freely, Sarah was able to express her sorrow fully and move through them quickly, without hijacking the mood of the whole house.

If a three year old can do it, so can you. That's how it works for all of us when we accept what we're feeling and allow ourselves to express it without harming anyone.

Releasing big energy is like opening a bottle of champagne.

In our busy but sedentary lives we have lots of stress, both good and bad, but few opportunities to burn it off.

Without expending the stress hormones through a physical response, they remain elevated in your body, building pressure and weighing you down. This creates a chronic state of distress and low level anxiety. Over time it can lead to depression and disease.

The explosion of all that pressure at once can be dangerous and messy.

You need simple and safe ways to release the energy inside.

Several of my overworked clients have discovered that underneath their constant busyness is a low-lying anxiety that's driving them. Some even find it's lurking under the weight of their depression.

It's often only when they begin to breathe and relax in our sessions that they notice this buzzing energy pushing them from within. They're sometimes shocked to discover this, but I can relate. I lived most of my life aware of my passions and desire to help others, and less aware of the underlying anxiety constantly feeding a belief that I could never do or be enough.

I encourage clients to release stress as soon as it happens, whenever possible, in little ways. Allowing for little releases throughout the day stops the pressure from building inside.

I invite them to notice their body's impulses, and then follow the impulse if that feels right. All of this can and must be done without ever harming themselves or another being.

Nicole and I hadn't been working together very long when I phoned her at our arranged time. She asked if I could give her five more minutes and call her back, so I did. Just before our session, she had been on a call with her health insurance provider about a billing dispute. (If you don't live in the US you can't appreciate the special hell it is to slog through issues with your health insurance company.)

Her insurance provider had been over-billing her. They were aware of the problem but hadn't corrected it. Her insurance was due soon and they told her to pay the overage again until they sorted the problem out at their end. Money was tight for her at the time. She was outraged and scared.

When I called her back her voice was strained. She apologized for the delay and wanted to get on with our coaching, but couldn't stop telling me the details of her call, and the problems that had led to it. I could totally understand her irritation.

I knew that talking about it wouldn't make the problem go away. Even if she switched to our coaching topic, she would have been forced to hold in that energy, building more pressure inside.

I asked her to feel her body and describe what was going on. She immediately noticed that her hands were in tight fists. I asked what else she felt.

She wanted to punch.

I encouraged her to follow that impulse. She stood up and began punching the air and grunting.

Within about 90 seconds she was done. She laughed. She was surprised by how light she felt. She had more energy. She was ready to start our coaching call.

Letting the energy out didn't change her billing problem. Talking about it incessantly wouldn't have changed it either. But letting her body react naturally, and express the energy that was building up inside, got her back into the present moment, full of energy and free of stress, happier, and ready to move on.

In some situations you can't follow an impulse. In that case, just feel the sensations of that impulse. Give it your attention as it transmutes.

If you've got the opportunity, close your eyes and imagine you're doing what your body wants to do. Slow it down so you can really feel it. Imagine yourself letting out a scream, running, punching, rocking, or whatever urge you feel. Just imagining this release can ease the pressure inside.

Your body knows how to release the energy. Your thoughts may get in the way.

We all push down our energy, only to find we can't stop talking or thinking about the problem.

When clients are stuck in an emotion and can't stop talking about an issue, I'll ask them to move the energy of their words through their body. They want to keep talking, because that's what we've all been taught to do, so I ask them to tell me everything they want to say in jibberish.

By speaking nonsense, they don't get stuck in the story. They just keep breathing and moving the energy. It provides relief from the thoughts that keep them stuck. Your thoughts are your biggest cause of stress and suffering. For simple ways to let go of stressful thoughts read Breathe.

Allowing and releasing works for more than just frustration and anger. Your joy, laughter, fear and excitement deserve the same attention. If you'll sense them and allow them to be, they'll move through you and allow you to feel much more.

It's important to note that if you have trauma, feeling sensations and letting your emotions flow can be overwhelming at first. It's important to get professional help. (Go to www.debrajoy.me/resources)

Start Moving.

Feelings are just energy, and moving directs it.

When I get clients moving they all do it in their own way. Some bounce on their feet. Some sway their arms back and forth. Some kick their legs in the air. Others dance. Some punch.

As they move, they get more in touch with their feelings, and eventually feel lighter, softer and more spacious. They always become more present.

You can do the same. Just get up and move in any way that feels good when pressure starts to build. It can help to make noise to ensure you're breathing.

If you know you need to release some energy, or at least you're willing to try, but you're not sure what to do, you might feel a little foolish. I totally get it. We're so used to living in our thoughts that we've lost connection with the wisdom of our bodies, so it may be hard to hear it.

Rather than get frustrated trying to figure out the right way to do it, you can start by shaking a bit.

If you've had to hold in emotions because it didn't feel appropriate to let them out, if you had a stressful day and can't let it go, if you're really excited and can't settle down, try shaking when you get somewhere private.

Picture a furry dog coming out of a lake. Its body's heavy with the weight of the water.

The very first thing it does when it reaches the shore is shake from head to tail. In 4 seconds that dog will shake 70% of the water off its body. If you're close by, most of it will no doubt land on you. After that quick shake, the dog's ready to run, walk, and play. If you leash a dog and try to rush it before it has a chance to shake, it'll stop and shake the first opportunity that it gets.

Without shaking that water off, the dog would waste up to 20% of his energy just to air dry. By shaking for 4 seconds the dog can use that energy for other things.

Keeping energy stuffed inside can weigh you down like a wet fur coat. The energy you gain by freeing yourself of denied feelings may be the difference between just surviving and thriving.

It can be a little shake, done quickly, maybe just your hands. If that feels good, you may want to do more. Include your arms and legs. Keep breathing while you're shaking. Make noise if that feels good.

Releasing your energy is like cleaning your house. Do it regularly.

If you've been overriding your feelings it can be a challenge to even notice them.

When you feel agitated, excited, or you're obsessing about something you can't let go, you're probably not going to think about releasing the energy because it's not normal for you.

You can teach yourself to release by making it a habit.

A few years ago I installed a drip irrigation system throughout our yard and vegetable garden. Once I was finished I had someone from the city come inspect it to make sure I had done it right. Just before he left he said, "Be sure to flush it out once a year." "Huh?" I didn't know what he was talking about.

"Even the tiniest bits of dirt will build up in your system and clog it up over time." he explained. "At least once a year, take the cap off the farthest end of the tubing. Turn the faucet on full blast and run the water through. This will clear out any debris and keep your system working properly".

A fleck of dirt on its own is no threat, but as bits of dirt gather together they block the system from working properly. We can say the same for your feelings.

One suppressed giggle, tear, or angry outburst isn't going to do much harm on its own. But over they years they build up like the pressure inside a champagne bottle. The weight of it keeps you from living as freely and effortlessly as you could.

Regular release can ease anxiety and bring peace.

Dave had great health and wealth. He was a loving and dedicated dad and husband, with close friends. He'd been working hard for decades building a business that served the community, and provided his family a wonderful life. He was proud of his accomplishments. Dave had every measure of external success, but his internal world was another story.

His thoughts were always racing, his mind full of lists he needed to complete. While taking care of one thing he'd think of something else he should be doing instead. He felt tightly wound. He blew up at his kids sometimes and felt terrible about it afterwards.

It took a lot of energy to contain the fire that burned inside.

He was searching for peace in his body and mind. He'd tried meditation but found it annoying. Yoga bored him.

I got Dave to drop the idea of what he should be doing to find peace, and we explored what his body wanted to do. Rather than work against his natural energy, we used it as a guide.

Though he hated to admit it, lots of times he wanted to punch the shit out of people.

He set up a heavy bag in his home gym. As soon as he came home from work he'd change into sweats, head downstairs and kick and punch out his frustrations from the day. He didn't always feel frustrated, but he felt like a weight was lifted from his shoulders every time he beat the bag. It cleared his mind. It became a great transition from his stressful workday to his home life.

Though he felt exhausted at first, he had more energy later in the evening for riding bikes with the kids or walking the dog with his wife.

Over time he noticed that his angry outbursts weren't happening as much. He was calmer in traffic, at work, and at home. Releasing the energy that needed to move, he was able to find peace.

You might find that if you release regularly for a while, it will become a habit. You'll create muscle memory.

Then you can use it any time you feel stress inside. The sooner you catch and release the sensations, the less opportunity there is for pressure to build.

It's important that you never aim the energy you release at another being. Even huge joy can shock them if the outburst is unexpected.

You'll feel more energized and alive.

Anger is a secondary emotion. We often feel it to cover up a more vulnerable feeling like fear or hurt.

Someone insults you in a meeting and you immediately pretend to feel nothing. You sit on your hurt. It keeps rising to the surface, and unconsciously that feels too vulnerable, so you switch to blaming the person, maybe even plotting your revenge.

When you allow the sensations to move through your body, rather than continue to feed an emotion with your thoughts, you get out from under the heaviness of lingering bitterness and resentment, and can release the more vulnerable feelings beneath.

That will free up a lot of energy that's been keeping you down. Just remember to feel the sensations in your body regularly, and allow them to move as soon as you can. That can be a challenge if your life is sedentary. See Move for ideas.

Energy release can be a part of your spiritual practice.

Releasing isn't a way of ridding yourself of anger, excitement, fear, or lust.

It's a way of accepting all those energies as a vibrant part of your human experience that don't define or limit who you are. They are an expression of divine energy moving through your body.

If all of this is very new to you, keep this in mind as you begin noticing sensations inside, and releasing them in whatever way feels right to you.

- Start very gently. Just noticing is enough.
- If you want to follow some impulses you feel in your body, do it in private, where you won't feel judged.
- Imagine following the impulse if you can't physically do it. Imagining doing it slowly.
- If you have a loving cohort who can be with you, encourage you, and make it easier for you, let them.
- Keep breathing and noticing, as you're releasing.
- Don't aim the energy at anyone else.
- Treat it lightly. Practice and explore. Have fun with it.

If you have a spiritual practice but still don't feel as free and joyful as you might, try incorporating awareness of sensations and regular release into your practice as an experiment. See what it does for you.

Sometimes to be able to sit quietly in meditation, flow through yoga, or devote yourself to service, you first need to release the tension inside by honoring what your body wants to do.

Releasing the energies inside will enable you to experience more of the vast peace and unbounded joy that are within you always.

If you accept and allow the energies inside you to be as they are and transmute as they will, you won't be run by your emotions. They won't determine the quality of your life.

You can experience sadness and still be joyful. You can feel fear and still be peaceful. You can have anger and still feel love. Because love, peace, and joy aren't just feelings you have, they're what you truly are.

RELEASE

Practices

– Sense What's Inside You –

It's enough just to feel sensations n your body. If you can allow and accept them without judgment, if you can be curious and open, you'll access the state of peace within you.

 Feel your feet on the ground. If you're sitting, feel your bum and the back of your legs touching the chair.

 Notice your body move with your breathing.

 See if you can feel any other sensations. If you do, just pay attention.

 Your mind will rush in with thoughts that will distract you. That's fine. Just bring your attention back to your body's sensations as soon as you notice you're up in your thoughts.

Some of the thoughts you think will be about your sensations, "This is good. This is bad. I don't want to feel this." Just notice the thoughts and bring your attention back to feeling your sensations.

If at any time your feelings are too much for you, notice your feet touching the floor. Let your eyes look around. Just notice what you see. You don't have to pay attention to sensations longer than feels right for you.

If you're overwhelmed by sensations in your body you can get help. (Go to www.debrajoy.me/resources.)

– WHAT'S UNDER YOUR EMOTIONS –

If you have trouble shifting from your emotions to your sensations, try this.

 Ask yourself, "how do I know I'm....(sad, happy, angry, scared...)

 Look for the sensations in your body that relate to that emotion.

 Just experience the sensations inside you. It may help to say what you feel.

 When you're done, feel your feet on the floor and just let your eyes look around. Notice how you feel.

You might notice that when you ask "how do I know?" your mind will rush in with reasons. I'm sad because my dog died. I'm happy because it's Sunday.

You don't have to do anything with those thoughts. Just allow them to come and go, as you focus on your body and notice the sensations inside.

You'll probably discover you're experiencing a lot more than just one feeling. And none of them last for very long. Each of them morphs into something different as you pay attention.

You don't have to give meaning to the sensations. Just noticing them will help you get beyond emotions and into your body's sensations. That will make you present.

– Immediate Release –

When you notice sensations inside you that you'd normally suppress, and you allow them to flow instead, you'll feel lighter and clearer.

 Notice your immediate response to push a sensation down. (It may be laughter, tears, a roar, etc.)

 Notice what it is your body wants to do.

 Allow that. Let your body express what wants to come out.

 If you can't allow it in the moment, imagine you're allowing it to move.

Always release your energy in a way that is safe for you and others.

Never aim your energy at another person. If you feel the need to punch, yell, kick, bite, or let loose in some wild way it's best to do it privately.

If you can't do it privately and safely, just imagine doing it slowly, so you can feel each part of the expression.

– QUICK FIX –

You're not always going to be able to feel your sensations and release emotions. Sometimes that's just not practical. When pressure is building inside you, try this practice that comes from Christopher Papadopoulos, author of Peace and Where to Find It.[49]

 Inhale as deeply as you can, then hold your breath.

 Clench every muscle in your body from face to toes.

 Hold this for a count of four.

 Exhale through your mouth slowly as you unclench your body.

If you have time you can do this four more times. It will relax your body and calm your mind. Chris's book, "Peace and Where to Find It" is a wonderful guide to the peace that is within you always. (You can get his book at www.debrajoy.me/resources)

– TIMELY RELEASE –

You can't always release your emotions in the moment that you feel them. Sometimes you won't even be able to do the Quick Fix.

When that happens it can be helpful to release your pent up sensations as soon as you get somewhere private.

 Feel your feet on the ground. Notice what you feel in your body.

 Let your body do whatever it wants to do. If you don't feel an impulse, just start moving gently. Maybe shake out your hands.

 Make noise if you can, to ensure you're breathing. If you can't make noise, just be sure to breathe.

 Stop after a few minutes. Notice how you feel.

You can repeat as many times as you like.

– REGULAR RELEASE –

Like vacuuming your rug, regular release takes care of the little bits of debris that collect throughout the day, before they have a chance to become a real mess.

 Make it a practice to release daily, until it becomes a habit.

 Set a timer for a few minutes, or play a song. It's best if the song has no words.

 Notice impulses in your body and follow them, the best you can. If you don't feel impulses, it can help to just start moving; dance, jump, shake, sway.

 When the timer goes or the song ends, feel your feet on the ground and notice how you feel.

You may not notice much of a difference after a few times of releasing, but over time you'll feel more freedom and spaciousness in your body.

While you may not have a need to release energy every day, doing it regularly will create a muscle memory so that when you're stressed you can remember to do this immediately.

Discontinue if doing this makes you feel worse.
(Go to www.debrajoy.me/resources)

– YOUR PRACTICE –

WHAT:

_____

Name this practice

WHY:

_____

_____

What do you expect to gain from this practice?
Knowing why you're doing it will help keep you motivated.

BREAK YOUR PRACTICE DOWN INTO VERY SIMPLE STEPS.

1. _____

_____

2. _____

_____

3. _____

_____

4. _____

_____

TRIGGER:

_____

When developing a new habit it's best to do it every day, at the same time if possible, and it's important to have something that reminds you, or triggers you to do it.

What will trigger you to do this practice?

- NOTES -

SUMMARY

This book is an invitation to know your true self beyond the ideas you have or stories you've been told about who you are and who you should be.

Each practice creates an opportunity to realize something more vast and profound. Something true.

I welcome you to incorporate these practices into your daily activities and let them act as a guide to a life more joyful, peaceful and powerful than you can possibly imagine.

If you've already been exploring the practices before getting to this page, you may be noticing some changes already.

If you haven't yet begun and don't know where to start, try the first chapter because everything begins with a breath.

In whichever chapter you begin, choose the practice that appeals to you most.

Make a habit of that practice.

Habits are best developed when they're performed daily, ideally at the same time. Try that for a month. Notice any changes. Then try it for a month longer. Notice changes and continue.

You've probably heard that it takes 28 days to form a new habit. It actually takes more time for most habits. So stick with the practices for longer. You'll probably see results quickly, and they'll grow as your practice increases.

Track your progress daily.

The simple act of writing down that you completed the practice will release dopamine in your nervous system, which is connected to feelings of pleasure and motivation. When you feel the effects of dopamine you're more likely to repeat the action because it feels good.

I've had clients experience profound shifts of consciousness in less than 90 days, with regular support.

I can't be with you to develop ideal practices in your life, or tweak things as we go to make sure you're getting what you need. Working with a book is a totally different deal than one on one coaching. And I'd like to support you as much as I can.

Join my Facebook Page where I can answer questions you might have.

www.facebook.com/ withdebrayjoy

I'm offering this with the hope that you'll experience the peace, joy, and love that you really are!

Love

Debra

A Big Fat Thank You!

I wouldn't have been able to complete this book without the love and support of a precious few. I'm so grateful for the way you've embraced my gifts and imperfections.

Deepest thanks to Nancy Bradshaw, my EBTAS, for your undying love and support; for reading each chapter with your whole body and generously reflecting it back to me with your whole heart. Your feedback made me a better writer. Your friendship makes me a better human.

Helene Zuckerman, thanks for always saying yes. For loving this work and defending it passionately. And for making me laugh until I cry. Jeff Sielaff, Master Flow and Buster, your quiet work in the background has made such a difference to me. I miss the sound of slurping water.

Thank you Bodhi Heart for wanting to share this with others before it was even written. Your trust and encouragement touch me. Thanks to my loving family for supporting the choices I've made that must seem crazy at times. It's wonderful to be accepted and loved just the way I am.

Steve Demelo, you're a dream to work with. I love your designs as much as I appreciate your patience.

Gerda Wever, I'm grateful for your kind-hearted editing and doggie rescuing. Cheryl Himmelstein, I love the way you see the world and capture it in photos. Thanks for your help with this work. Elizabeth Grojean, Dawn Cartwright, Sonia Keshishian and Onyay Pheori, thank you for the gifts of your beauty and time. You helped bring this to life. Chris Papadopoulos, you're truly a man of peace, with a generous heart, and a keen eye for detail.

I'm deeply grateful to my clients. Your courage and dedication to living fully excites and touches me. It's an honor to be a small part of your journey. Thank you for allowing me.

Thank you to all the teachers who've guided me whether you meant to or not. Being brave enough to speak your truth and share your gifts has inspired me, even if I didn't know it at the time.

Mark Schwartz, I love you for joining me in this life, supporting me more than anyone will ever know, and laughing with me through it all. Thanks for being brave enough to tell me I needed to start again at the beginning, when I thought I was finished. "You were right!" I probably don't say that enough.

Notes

[1] Levine, P. A. (1997). *Waking the tiger: Healing trauma.* Berkeley: North Atlantic Books.

[2] Perls, F. S. (1973). *The gestalt approach & Eye witness to therapy.* Ben Lomond: Science & Behavior Books.

[3] Stone, L. (2014, November 24). Screen apnea. Retrieved from https://lindastone.net/tag/screen-apnea

[4] Lowen, A. (1990). *The spirituality of the body: Bioenergetics for grace and harmony.* New York: Macmillan. 1990

[5] Lowen, A., & Lowen, L. (1977). *The way to vibrant health: A manual of bioenergetic exercises.* Alachua: Bioenergetics Press.

[6] Bowman, K. (2014). *Move your DNA: Restore your health through natural movement.* Sequim: Propriometrics Press.

[7] Montagu, A. (1971). *Touching: The human significance of the skin.* New York: Harper & Row.

[8] Heller, S. (1997). *The vital touch: How intimate contact with your baby leads to happier, healthier development.* New York: Henry Holt.

[9] Linden, D. J. (2015). *Touch: The science of hand, heart, and mind.* New York: Penguin Books.

[10] Dworkin-McDaniel, N. (2011, January 5). Touching makes you healthier. Retrieved from http://www.cnn.com/2011/HEALTH/01/05/touching.makes.you.healthier.health

[11] Bakalar, N. (2009, August 10). Five-second touch can convey specific emotion, study finds. Retrieved from http://www.nytimes.com/2009/08/11/science/11touch.html?_r=0

[12] Guerrero, L. K., Andersen, P. A., & Afifi, W. A. 2014 *Close encounters: Communication in relationships.* Los Angeles: Sage Publications.

[13] Song, S. (2010, June 24). Study: How things you touch influence the way you think. Retrieved from http://healthland.time.com/2010/06/24/study-how-things-you-touch-influence-the-way-you-think

[14] Williams, L. E., & Bargh, J. A. (2008). Experiencing physical warmth promotes interpersonal warmth. Science, 322(5901), 606-607. Retrieved from http://science.sciencemag.org/content/322/5901/606.full

[15] Kraus, M. W., Huang, C., & Keltner, D. (2010). Tactile communication, cooperation, and performance: An ethological study of the NBA. *Emotion, 10*, 745-749. Retrieved from http://socrates.berkeley.edu/~keltner/publications/kraus.touch.2010.pdf

[16] DeSteno, D. (2015, July 21). How mindfulness meditation builds compassion. Retrieved from http://www.theatlantic.com/health/archive/2015/07/mindfulness-meditation-empathy-compassion/398867

[17] Binns, C. (2006, May 22). How we smell things: A guide to the human nose. Retrieved from http://www.livescience.com/10457-smell.html

[18] Stromberg, J. (2015, August 27). What science says about meditation: It improves your focus and emotional control. Retrieved from http://www.vox.com/2015/8/27/9214697/meditation-brain-neuroscience

[19] Corliss, J. (2015, February 18). Mindfulness meditation helps fight insomnia, improves sleep. Retrieved from http://www.health.harvard.edu/blog/mindfulness-meditation-helps-fight-insomnia-improves-sleep-201502187726

[20] Epel, E. S., McEwen, B., Seeman, T., Matthews, K., Castellazzo, G., Brownell, K. D., Bell J., Ickovics, J. R. (2000). Stress and body shape: Stress-induced cortisol secretion is consistently greater among women with central fat. Psychosomatic Medicine, 62(5), 623-632.

[21] Berke, J. D., & Hyman, S. E. (2000). Addiction, dopamine, and the molecular mechanisms of memory. Neuron, 25(3), 515-532.

[22] Gould, T. J. (2010). *Addiction and cognition. Addiction Science & Clinical Practice, 5(2)*, 4-14. Retrieved from http://www.ncbi.nlm.nih.gov/pmc/articles/PMC3120118

[23] Hyman, M. (2014). *The blood sugar solution: The ultrahealthy program for losing weight, preventing disease, and feeling great now!* New York: Little, Brown and Co.

[24] McGonigal, K. (2012). *The willpower instinct: How self-control works, why it matters, and what you can do to get more of it.* New York: Penguin Group

[25] Schmidt, E. (2012, May 15). This is your brain on sugar: UCLA study shows high-fructose diet sabotages learning, memory. Retrieved from http://newsroom.ucla.edu/releases/this-is-your-brain-on-sugar-ucla-233992

[26] Ratey, J. J., & Hagerman, E. (2008). *Spark: The revolutionary new*

science of exercise and the brain. New York: Little, Brown.

[27] Ratey, J. J., & Manning, R. (2014). *Go wild: Free Your Body and Mind from the Afflictions of Civilization*. New York: Little, Brown.

[28] Bowman, K. (2014). *Move your DNA: Restore your health through natural movement*. Sequim: Propriometrics Press.

[29] Khazan, O. (2014, November 18). What texting does to the spine. Retrieved from http://www.theatlantic.com/health/archive/2014/11/what-texting-does-to-the-spine/382890

[30] *Amy Cuddy: Your body language shapes who you are* [Video file]. (2012). Retrieved from http://www.ted.com/talks/amy_cuddy_your_body_language_shapes_who_you_are

[31] Kabat-Zinn, J. (1994). Wherever you go, there you are: *Mindfulness meditation in everyday life*. New York: Hyperion.

[32] Dispenza, J. (2014). *You are the placebo: Making your mind matter*. Carlsbad: Hay House, Inc.

[33] *Continuum Movement*. (n.d.). Retrieved from http://continuummovement.com

[34] Selhub, E. M., & Logan, A. C. (2012). *Your brain on nature: The science of nature's influence on your health, happiness and vitality*. Mississauga: John Wiley & Sons Canada.

[35] Jensen, F. E., & Nutt, A. E. (2015). *The teenage brain: A neuroscientist's survival guide to raising adolescents and young adults*. New York: Harper.

[36] Jung, C.G. (1968) Man and His Symbols. New York: Dell Publishing.

[37] Copinschi G. (2005). Metabolic and endocrine effects of sleep deprivation. *Essential Psychopharmacology*, 6(6), 341-347. Retrieved from http://europepmc.org/abstract/med/16459757

[38] Loehr, J. E. (1995). *The new toughness training for sports: Mental, emotional, and physical conditioning from one of the world's premier sports psychologists*. New York: The Penguin Group.

[39] Ferriss, T. (2007). *The 4-hour workweek: Escape 9-5, live anywhere, and join the new rich*. New York: Crown Publishers.

[40] Moller, K. (2015, December 31). *The need for zzzz*. Retrieved from https://smith.queensu.ca/insight/articles/the_need_for_zzzz

[41] Huffington, A. (2014). *Thrive: the third metric to redefining success and creating a life of well-being, wisdom, and wonder*. New York: Harmony Books.

[42] Mednick, S. C. (2006). *Take a nap!: Change your life*. New York: Workman Publishing.

[43] Maas, J. B. (1998). *Power sleep: The revolutionary program that prepares your mind for peak performance*. New York: Villard.

[44] Rettner, R. (2011, March 10). *Nighttime gadget use interferes with young adults' health*. Retrieved from http://www.livescience.com/35536-technology-sleep-adolescents.html

[45] Edlund, M. (2011). *The power of rest: Why sleep alone is not enough : a 30-day plan to reset your body*. New York: HarperOne.

[46] LeDoux, J. (1998). *The emotional brain: The mysterious underpinnings of emotional life*. New York: Simon & Schuster.

[47] Abrams, J., & Zweig, C. (Eds.). (1991). *Meeting the shadow: The hidden power of the dark side of human nature*. New York: J.P. Tarcher.

[48] Jung, C. G. (1957). *The undiscovered self*. New York: Signet.

[49] Papadopoulos, C. (2015). *Peace: And where to find it*. Vancouver: Namaste Publishing.

Made in the USA
San Bernardino, CA
31 October 2017